LEANING ON M

LEANING ON
MOM

Letters to Roberta

HOW A MOM OF THREE BOYS
WITH AUTISM FOUND STRENGTH
DURING THE PANDEMIC

MELANIE DONUS
FOREWORD BY: RAY CEPEDA, BCABA, CBAA

MelanieDonus.com

This book is dedicated to me and the other millions of moms with a child on the Autism spectrum. Each of us are working through our own challenges, some struggling to meet their child's needs at home, and others with children in group homes who haven't seen each other in months due to the coronavirus quarantine pandemic regulations.

It may seem narcissistic to some to dedicate a book to myself, but Roberta would be super proud of me for putting myself first for once.

TABLE OF CONTENTS

Foreword   1

Introduction   5

Cast of Characters   7

Letters to Roberta   15

Epilogue   119

FOREWORD

$\mathcal{J}$ust about everyone has or knows someone who has a family member with autism. People who don't know anything about autism are "aware" of autism due to the many successful marketing campaigns and celebrities that are attached to "awareness." Autism is so prevalent that people who do not even have children with autism have opinions about such controversial topics as vaccines, treatments, or that a parent can fix their child's behavior with a good "kick in the pants." Well, as someone who has been collaborating with families for over two and a half decades, I feel confident saying that I have seen what our autism parents experience every day. I have seen the pain, frustration, anxiety, exhaustion, happiness, joy, exhilaration, and delight that these parents experience (sometimes all in the same day!). The parents that I am fortunate to have the opportunity to work with are so dedicated to their children's success that their determination motivates me every day to partner with them to help them help their children.

When Melanie asked me to write the foreword for her book, I immediately said, "Yes!" Even though I didn't even know what her book was about! Sometimes you just have to jump in feet first, right? Then, she told me about the structure of her book, written as letters to her mother about her everyday experiences with her three sons with autism. I was fascinated. Why? Because no one really knows what goes on with our autism parents, no one really "gets" it, and while this book may be just one mother's experience, I strongly feel that it is vital for the readers to have some insight into the life of one autism mom. Autism is twenty-four/seven . . . for life. Autism does not take vacations, it does not take breaks, and sometimes it doesn't sleep, and when autism is not sleeping, neither are our autism parents. Now, many of you may be saying, "My kid doesn't have autism, but my kid doesn't sleep sometimes, they're a picky eater, and they can have tantrums, and they can be challenging. What's the big deal?" I've had people say these things to me when they find out what I do. The only response I can offer to such ridiculous comments is, "You have no idea." And honestly, neither do I. What I know of what our autism parents do, feel, and experience daily barely scratches the surface.

When COVID-19 forced everyone to stay at home, I immediately thought about Melanie and her three boys, who are quite different but who all need their routines, structure, education, treatments, and therapists. Suddenly, Melanie had to be all those things to all three boys.

We all realize that the pandemic hit just about everyone hard, but again, unless you have a child with developmental differences, you probably don't get it (but you will!). I don't think that Melanie's main concern was stocking-up on toilet paper. Well . . . maybe a little, after all, five people are living in her house! One of her first feelings was panic when she thought about school being cancelled for months and her home-based therapists no longer coming to the house. I am also sure she felt overwhelmed thinking about regression, aggressive behavior, toilet training, teaching her son to use his communication device as well as a thousand other things that would have to get handled every day so that her boys could feel even a little settled. When was she supposed to grab a two-minute shower? As I said, you have no idea.

Melanie's life is not only focused on her boys, but she has had some serious personal challenges to overcome (read the book to find out more, this is the foreword, not Cliff's Notes!). So, please avoid reading this book just for the sake of reading. Don't read this book because you have an "I wonder what it's like . . ." curiosity; this is not entertainment, it's Melanie's life. The life of one parent with three children with autism. Think about that, *feel that*. What happens in your body when you focus on those words, "three children with autism"?

As you read this book, I want you to feel what Melanie felt when she wrote it. So, before you pick up this book, take three slow deep breaths and clear your mind, and then begin reading and focus on the narrative, feel the emotions behind the words, visualize what Melanie is writing. When your mind starts to wander, stop, take a breath, and remind yourself that this is Melanie's life, not some work of fiction that allows you to stay emotionally detached and that you can forget and discard after you put the book down. Then, refocus on the book. Once you are done with the book, call that friend from college whom you lost touch with who has a child with autism, and tell her that you "kinda get it."

Ray Cepeda, BCaBA, CBAA
Founder and Director, ABAskills, LLC
www.abaskills.com
Co-founder, 121 Learning Works

INTRODUCTION

$\mathcal{B}$e kind. The 2020 COVID-19 pandemic created a world unlike any of us imagined, and there will be ripple effects of this time for decades to come. My heartfelt condolences go out to those who lost loved ones during this pandemic. I pray that God will wrap his arms of comfort and love around the families of deceased coronavirus victims. May their memories be eternal.

I wrote this book to share my own personal experience as a mother of three school-aged children with Autism Spectrum Disorder during the initial four months of the 2020 coronavirus pandemic. Remember, I am just one mother, a very proud yet humble one at that. While you may see terms such as "ASD Mom" within these pages, terms like these are not meant to be a label; I am simply Dimitri, Michael, and Maxx's Mom. My three loves of my life, my boys, happen to have autism.

Often a single day at home with a child with autism without getting them out of the house can seem like an eternity for both the child and the parent. In the same vein, another day without seeing your child in a group home, being quarantined without you for over three months due to COVID-19 restrictions, is unfathomable. This period in time has set the bar to an all-new high for families to figure out how to muddle through.

Please, I ask that you be extra kind to an ASD Mom if you see her in the community over the next few months as all of us will need recovery time — physically, mentally, and spiritually. That mother you see most likely felt a new loneliness like she never knew existed during this time, even if quarantined with a husband, wife, or significant other. Getting "back to normal" is not in our vocabulary, and the pandemic has brought a new meaning to the words "rise to the occasion." Many parents feel like they ran an intense marathon with an ever changing finish line that they didn't train for or even know was coming; their bodies and minds are in shock and dismay.

May this book not only bring more awareness to the unique challenges of ASD but also appreciation of the resilience of children with autism and awe of the strength and courage amongst all of their families during this time.

Amongst the millions of pandemic stories and experiences shared by people across the world, this is mine.

CAST OF CHARACTERS

MEL – That's me, and I am married to Andrew. I am known for my ability to advocate for my three boys with autism, Michael and Dimitri (twins, age 17), and Maxx (age 12). I am passionate about giving back to the autism community, and I volunteer frequently for a local Long Island charitable organization and have been known to coordinate "special projects" to support local families in crisis. Prior to having our third child, Maxx, I held an executive role at a recognizable global investment bank, and before the COVID-19 outbreak, I spent the last decade in my home office juggling administration for the boys' programs while serving as VP at a boutique executive recruiting agency.

On the outside, I may look completely put together (outside of quarantine time or baseball hat days), but I secretly struggle with alcoholism.

ANDREW – My supportive, loving husband and father to the three boys. Andrew holds a visible title as a Senior VP at a global investment bank in Manhattan and has a long, two-hour commute each way from Long Island to the World Financial Center. He does his best to keep up with all of the autism-related acronyms used constantly in our home, but his main role in our household is that of the breadwinner. Quiet and stoic, he never stops making me laugh with his surprising, sometimes twisted, dry sense of humor. He is known as Daddio to the boys and is a die-hard Yankees and Giants fan. He loves to watch the Food Network channel, and we cherish our alone time together on Friday nights eating leftovers while watching *Diners, Drive-Ins and Dives*. Thank God it's not football season during quarantine because we watch our usual Sunday afternoon favorite show, *Impractical Jokers*, while he prepares our usual Sunday evening dinner of grilled salmon and Greek lemon potatoes.

MICHAEL – One of my teen twins, sweet and charming. Michael has terrific language, and his technology skills surpass his cognitive level on paper. He is capable of getting through firewalls and servers with multiple layers of passwords. He is practically a walking Wiggles Wikipedia page and is obsessed with owning every single Wiggles item there is available for purchase, sorted by manufacturing date, country, and any identifiable object on the packaging that makes them fall into the "different" category. He owns literally tens of thousands of dollars in Wiggles memorabilia and is an active participant in multiple platforms on social media for Wiggles international fan groups. He plays Roblox frequently in The Wiggly Robloxicans team where they build Wiggles concerts, stages, and playgrounds. His interactions online have created some deep-level relationships with other Wiggles fans.

Michael is mostly challenged by OCD and non-compliance behavior issues. The local police precinct is called to the house frequently, often resulting in him being transported to the local hospital, usually in high-anxiety situations when Michael is fixating on items he does not yet own. He has been accepted to an out-of-state therapeutic residential school and was ready to attend in early April before the COVID-19 outbreak. Andrew and I are hopeful he can learn coping mechanisms and effective life skills so that he can return and live what's called a "self-directed" life in New York. Michael attends a local high school program in a classroom with an innovative autism program and is considered an exceptional student and a "joy to be around" by his teachers, and he is 100% compliant with them. He thrives in a highly structured environment, and problematic behaviors only occur in our home or when we are with him in the community. While Andrew and I do our best to provide the most structured household as possible, downtime naturally happens while at home, along with unexpected changes and interruptions from his brothers.

DIMITRI – Our other teen twin, whose nickname is Teddybear! Generally loving and compliant, he has a lot of language and loves Instagram, described as his "messenger with teenage friends." He loves taking photos and is obsessed with Times Square and theater. His behavior plan enables him to earn money that he uses to purchase playbills, and he has more than five leather binders with each playbill perfectly organized. He loves attending school and his after-school activities, including theater club, hip-hop dance, weekly bowling, and participating in the Long Island All Star Athletics program where his classmates compete with other students with disabilities in various sports. He also works at a local Italian restaurant where he folds to-go pizza boxes. He is passionate about gardening and baking and quite talented at cake decorating, and he says that he wants to work at a bakery in Manhattan after high school graduation.

Dimitri fixates on times, schedules, and routines, and he struggles on the weekends and periods of school vacation time when the schedule is flexible. It becomes challenging for him if he doesn't know when you are coming and going, down to the very minute, and he likes to check receipts when I come home from errands to confirm that I am being honest about when I arrived at and left places. He has a photographic memory, remembers strange details from specific dates years ago, and frequently uses Google Maps to confirm how long I should be gone based on where I said I was going.

Dimitri loves socializing and spending time with his cousins during the holidays or family celebrations; he counts down the days and specific times until he sees them from event to event. He attends the same local high school program as Michael but is in a separate classroom during a few periods a day. He is very popular at school and the general education students are so incredibly kind and supportive when interacting with him.

MAXX – Our youngest son, age 12. He has the most angelic face and requires the most support of the three boys. A giggle box, he is always smiling. Maxx is non-verbal but tries very hard to speak — he also suffers from apraxia of speech and uses an iPad to communicate. Maxx loves giving hugs, and teachers can't get enough of him. A few teachers have said that it would be hard to teach him all day because he is so loving and cute. Maxx's favorite thing in the world is the ocean, with the close second and third favorites being swinging and taking long drives with "house music" playing loudly in the background. He breaks into a celebration when "Peanut Butter Jelly" by Galantis comes on and shrieks with laughter and bops his head all around when he hears it. His favorite TV Shows are The Masked Singer and Ellen's Game of Games, and we use those as rewards in between learning tasks.

Maxx is talented at playing puzzle games on the computer and is showing a big interest in using technology like the rest of the family. He attends a specialized center-based program for children with autism on Long Island where he learns using the ABA (Applied Behavior Analysis) method and discrete trial learning. He comes home after a 50-minute bus ride to a 2-hour schedule of at home instructions with various teachers and therapists. He is often described as the class clown and the happiest child that professionals have ever worked with.

DONNA - My code name for my friend and confidant, chardonnay.

ROBERTA – My mom. She was my rock, my comic relief, and a very devout Christian. I inherited her advocacy skills after watching Roberta and my dad parent my brother, Michael, who was born with a genetic defect that caused significant physical and cognitive disabilities. Her passion for children with disabilities began when my brother was born, and before she retired, she worked as a one-to-one teacher's aide for a little girl in a wheelchair, whom she lifted multiple times a day. My mom loved drinking coffee while reading anything centered around faith, prayer, and inspiration, including books authored by Grace Livingston Hill and *Guidepost* magazine.

Roberta was never afraid to speak her unsolicited and sometimes inappropriate opinion, quite often at awkward times like in a supermarket line to the customer behind her about their choice of tattoos and body piercings or in an elevator about someone's flip flops. Roberta was very dedicated to her church and attended multiple times per week and was a member of the ladies' prayer group. She received an honorary award from her church in 2016 for never missing or being one minute late to her Wednesday night Awana class, where she taught Bible classes to children. She was known for being a caregiver to shut-ins and terminally ill people and enjoyed visiting nursing homes even though she, herself, walked with a walker and drove a car with gas and brake hand controls. My mom loved feminine fashion, particularly with the colors pink and purple; she never went anywhere without her pink lipstick and a spritz of Estee Lauder Youth Dew perfume.

LETTERS TO ROBERTA

Dear Roberta,

What a week! I didn't feel very good at physical therapy on Saturday and had to walk outside to clear my throat because I didn't want to bring attention to it. On Sunday, the cough got worse, and I felt achy. I took a few hours to sit on the couch and watch Law and Order before we started the Sunday night ritual of getting everyone prepared to go to school on Monday. You know that sitting is something that I rarely do, but I felt exhausted.

Oh, how I wish that you could have been in NY in December and January when we admitted Michael into a special hospital for autistic behaviors two weeks before Christmas. It was such a challenging decision and having him hospitalized out-of-state during Christmas was painful to say the least. During his hospitalization, Michael's medication was changed, and he was given a list of rules that must be adhered to when he got home. Well, he adhered to his promise of taking the bus for an entire three weeks but then regressed back to refusing to ride, so now we have a fabulous autism consultant, Dan, who comes to our home three days a week solely for the bus routine.

Dan arrives every morning at 6:30 to make sure that Michael gets up, adheres to the morning routine, and gets on the bus. THANK GOD for Dan, who could never make a mistake in my eyes. He has been such a support for me, and I know that you would be so grateful for him too.

My cough has worsened, and it made me a little nervous on Monday, but I shook it off, and Dan came into the house and got Michael off to school. As the day went by, I started to feel worse, so I cancelled all after-school teachers who usually come to our house out of precaution that I might have a cold.

I am dreading Friday, Mom. I have the meeting that every autism mom hopes that they never have to attend — the meeting to finalize their child's residential school placement. After scouring NY State, we have decided that an out-of-state school is the best for him, and I know that we are making the best decision. I break into tears every time that I think about telling him. It's going to shatter me, Mom — I don't know how I can actually do it since I can barely even write about it. He is just so capable, and this school has a reputation for transforming non-compliant students with ASD and his profile.

Even though I know the plans have been made, sitting around a conference room table finalizing it all is going to make this very real, and I don't know how I am going to hold it all together. I will just keep telling myself, "You can cry in the car; you can cry in the car." I wish that you could come with me so much. At least Andrew is working virtually from home now for a few weeks, so he can go with me. I secretly wish it were you instead 😊.

Love,

Optimistically Overwhelmed

Dear Roberta,

Wow! What a difference a few days makes.

Well . . . now I feel even worse, and I had to hold the dreaded meeting virtually in my van. I spoke to my doctor yesterday, and she told me to "act as if I have the virus" and self-quarantine for fourteen days. My mind is racing, but I am not afraid of this virus. I am more afraid of the quarantine.

At the end of the meeting today, I was asked to stay on for a short private call. I kind of knew what was coming but was hoping that perhaps it was for a "pick me up" support message. I fell apart when I was told that the district's stance on parents who are self-quarantined like me is to keep their children at home for fourteen days as well.

Mom, I am disappointed in myself because I didn't respond in the stoic way that you would. I cried, I begged, I cursed. I remember saying in my voice that could barely speak, "Please don't do this to me!" All I could think about was being at home for fourteen days straight with the boys. How would I tell them that they weren't going to school, yet everyone else was? How would I live for Christ's sake?

Fourteen straight days without going anywhere? I just kept thinking to myself, "Are they f'ing kidding me? They can't be serious!"

I sensed that the district may be genuinely worried for my wellbeing and that I could have spread the virus to the village of teachers and staff that the district has so kindly put in place for me. I felt so guilty as if I had contracted something dirty, and I felt irresponsible because I had sent the boys to school when I was sick. I explained that there is a limited number of tests and my physician had been advised to only give tests to senior citizens, those who have underlying health risks, and those who have traveled internationally or have been in contact with someone who has a confirmed case of the virus. There seemed to be silence at the other end of the phone and I felt obligated to somehow, someway get tested for both mine and their comfortability. The district has helped my family immeasurably and I wanted to do anything I could to set their minds at ease.

I started calling everywhere trying to get tested, and the answer was always no. I finally did what my physician's staff told me not to do; I drove to their office and demanded that I get tested. Period. I have all of the symptoms, and I could possibly wipe out an entire school of teachers, so I couldn't accept no for an answer. My thoughts went to a pregnant teacher who was in contact with me and a teaching assistant who is a caregiver to a senior loved one when not at work. This is just horrible! I am incredibly sick myself, trying to wrap my head around the fact that I have to keep my children, who have ASD, at home for fourteen days in the house, and I am begging for a coronavirus test. I feel more concerned for others than for my own health, yet for once in my life, I am trying to intentionally take the steps necessary to take care of myself. How am I supposed to get better with all of them at home?

Well Mom, your lessons in practicing persistence worked. After arriving at the doctor's office, I was administered two different tests, and then I called the school to give them the comfort of knowing they would soon know for certain if I had exposed them to the virus. The staff could make the decision for themselves to self-quarantine or not until I received the results. As I drove home in the pouring rain, fear started to settle in, and my mind wouldn't stop racing.

I have to stay home for fourteen days, and staff might have to stay home unless my test is negative. I hope everyone doesn't find out that it is me. I hope that the district doesn't close down because of me. The district Director of Student Affairs called me and had to conduct an interview with me while I was driving home because she is required to report my self-quarantine to the Department of Health.

I arrived home and collapsed onto the couch because my fever was starting to spike again. Twenty minutes later, Dimitri, who is always aware of school news hours before me (LOL), came upstairs and announced that our school district is closed for two weeks. I seriously cannot believe that I just went through five hours of this intense emotional roller coaster for nothing. At least, I find comfort in that I don't have to explain that the boys have to stay home because I am sick, a new norm, which would most certainly lead to a lifetime of questions every time that I show a slight sniffle.

Mom, I am so exhausted mentally, physically and spiritually by the end of the day. If you were here, I would have avoided telling you about today as it happened because you would have been so sad for me. I know that you would have called me and asked, "How was your meeting?" and I would have responded, "It wasn't as bad as I thought." Then, you would ask how I am feeling because I sound so horrible, and I would tell you that I am OK and taking Tylenol Cold and taking care of myself. I would never have told you that I had to get tested for the virus. I also would have never told you that I drank a tremendous amount of chardonnay that night despite being sick.

Love,

Your Tested, Tough, and
Temporal Daughter

Dear Roberta,

Oh boy, Roberta! I think that a lot of people are feeling relieved today because I only have a strain of the flu, and now, I have also developed pneumonia. Yay for me.

Dimitri is really having a hard time understanding all of this. I was given a great social story from one of our autism behavior consultants to help explain coronavirus to a child with ASD. It seems to help him a little. Michael couldn't care less. I mean really, Mom — he is in heaven because he doesn't have to go to school for two weeks. My heart is breaking for Maxx who is starting to show symptoms. His pediatrician agreed to see us because I tested negative. He tells me to just keep watching him.

I keep watching Maxx as instructed — morning, noon, and night. Mom, I can't tell you how incredibly exhausted I am. I am trying to get better, and Maxx wants me to sit on the couch beside him all day. He isn't sleeping at all and is almost demon-like with multiple meltdowns that wake up the entire house every night. This is a Maxx that we have never seen because he is usually the happiest child in the world. It seems like the lights are on in our house all night every night, and I am surprised that no one has called the police from the screaming — screaming from Maxx's meltdowns that result in screaming from Michael to tell him to shut the F up because he is trying to sleep. Dimitri keeps practicing his breathing and hasn't hit the top of his tolerance scale yet; thank God because that's when it gets super ugly — when all three of them are escalated. That has never happened in the middle of the night before, only in the daytime when I at least have some form of energy. Really God? Mom, please, if you can talk to him or anyone that can intervene, please do so immediately.

I am so exhausted that I can barely dial the pediatrician, and he tells me to come back. He agrees to treat Maxx for an ear infection even though his ears need to be irrigated badly, which could also be causing pressure on his eardrums, and that procedure of course requires sedation for him. Wow. How am I supposed to find someone to do this in a pandemic?

I went home and called every ENT that I know to see if their office sedation suites were open, but no dice. Out of desperation, I posted it on the local Mom's group and of course I got a hit. BOOM! He has an appointment on Friday to see an ENT that has an internal sedation suite that's still open. Please God, give Maxx and me some relief.

I am so tired, but I need to make dinner and start the bedtime rituals. I know that tomorrow I must try to get some kind of homeschool program together for Dimitri. First, I need wine. A lot of wine.

Love,

Sleepless and Barely Sane

MARCH 20, 2020

Dear Roberta,

Governor Cuomo just announced that non-essential stores will close on Monday. It's almost as if you tapped his staff on the shoulder and told them to include liquor stores on the non-essential list. You are absolutely right in that this ship is going to go down if I try to manage whatever THIS is with "Donna," a daily bottle (or two) of chardonnay, in my hand. She helps melt the day away, and I often feel like she is the only "person" that truly understands me.

Mom, I remember when you called me after our last visit together in Pennsylvania and asked me how much time I spend with Donna. You reminded me that my dad had a similar friend that almost killed him. I listened to you three years ago when you told me that you were concerned about my relationship with her and that it may be toxic. Yes, I felt much better then, and my liver fell in love with me again. You were right then, and you are right now, but something is telling me that our breakup is not going to be as simple and clean-cut as the last time. The last time, I surrounded myself with other friends in the same room who recently had similar breakups; I even had a supportive therapist and was able to cry, scream, and have private discussions about my co-dependence and fear of rebound.

Mom, I continuously ask myself why I do not have the ability to keep a healthy relationship on track with her. Why do Donna and I have such a roller coaster friendship? Nevertheless, I accept that once again my friendship with her has run its course.

I am expecting the acute loneliness that I felt in our first breakup. I remember being counseled to find another engaging activity during the time that I usually spent with her. Hmmm, let me think now. We spent a lot of time together, sometimes starting around 5:00 p.m., or earlier depending upon the day. Now, that's a big chunk of time to find another engaging activity within the walls of this tiny three-bedroom ranch house rental.

Mom, I am going to miss her companionship so much, so I have to spend as much time as I can with her before D-Day. I hope that you understand my plans to enjoy every minute of time with her that I can until I call our relationship quits again. Please know that I will be safe, and I am one hundred percent committed to starting the path to health again on Monday, during the beginning of what is predicted to be the worst pandemic in the world in one hundred years. Why the hell am I listening to you??? These days, I can't get through a snow day or a weekend without Donna, and now, I am supposed to just cut her off, cold turkey? Yes, I will listen again, but please remember what I have always told you time and time again: I am still the boss of me, not you 😊.

Love,

*Defiant and
Determined Daughter*

Dear Roberta,

It's here. We are all at home for an indefinite period of time. I don't know how to explain this to Dimitri and Michael. My heart is going to break for Maxx because I can't explain it to him. How am I going to manage Dimitri if I don't have concrete answers about daily schedule changes? Remember, he falls apart if the bus is one minute late or refuses to get on the bus if it arrives one minute early. Michael refuses to take his medicine from either me or Andrew — what happens if he is off? What happens if he has one of his epic meltdowns? Will he attempt to hurt us or himself? What happens if the police take him to the hospital? Will they even take him to the hospital? How can I get him to go to sleep at night without medication?

Words cannot explain how panicked and fearful I am for what may unfold in the days ahead. There's a part of me that's glad that you aren't here because I know that you would worry yourself sick, yet there's a part of me that wants my mom so badly. As a mom myself, I have walked through a lot of challenges surrounding the boys' autism-related disabilities, but this, Mom, has a huge possibility of downright breaking me.

It would be so much easier if I had a crystal ball and knew how long this would last. School is cancelled for two weeks, and the professionals are all advising parents with the same guidance: stick to a schedule. OK, I will give this a one hundred percent try. After all, I have schedules all over my house. Half of my kitchen is in blackboard paint with a bi-monthly calendar and weekly schedules broken down by each child, staff member, teacher, and therapist, sometimes down to the minute for Dimitri. Now that I think about it, perhaps this won't be that challenging for me.

Three days without my girl. I have thought of her from time to time, but after the first twenty-four hours without her, combined with distractions, I have successfully achieved a few days of sobriety again. Yay me, but the days have been relatively smooth without autism-related behavior challenges, so I tend to discount my recent success. I'm not feeling too confident, but I'm taking it day by day. Leaning on my friend Karen who, aside from Andrew and you, Mom, is the only person who knows that I slipped. There I said it. I slipped from sobriety for two long years. Karen is cheering me on, but Donna keeps calling and somehow I am finding the strength to press decline.

Love,

Terrified and Trying to Abstain

Dear Roberta,

OMG, Mom. The moment my feet hit the floor in the morning, I head for the coffee, and then I suddenly find myself crawling into bed 15 hours later. We are only a few days into the Cuomo-mandated quarantine, and I am speechless. No school, no staff, no support, no Donna, and I can't see you.

We have discovered how to hide Michael's medicine in yogurt. I can't get all of it in throughout the day, but he is getting the two most important ones out of the grand total of five. If I have to dispense his emergency medication for severe behavior meltdowns, I will try to hide it discreetly in his ice cream. I know that he is going to see me one day or figure this out, and then the shit is really going to hit the fan. So far so good though, other than shouting and cursing so loudly that you can hear it down the street, threatening to break the windows, and slamming the microwave door so hard that it sounds like it is going to disintegrate into a million pieces. All of this stops if we give in to his demands, which are usually surrounding getting access to an item that he saw on social media somewhere. We have been ordering items for days of good behavior, and I send them to the behavior consultants' office because I don't want items randomly being delivered to our home. His anxiety is through the roof now about these items and how he is going to get them now that everything is closed. I don't know the answer to that question myself.

Mom, I feel so guilty for biting your head off every time that you suggested that I just cut Michael off of social media. At seventy-seven years old, you continued to ask me because you would forget my answer: I can't cut Michael off of the internet because of Dimitri. Remember that Dimitri has soared by using social media, and he uses it properly. He has self-developed the most impressive communication, research, and self-teaching skills. If I cut Michael off of the internet, I would have to cut Dimitri off too, and I simply won't do that to him.

Love,

Your Juggling and Far From
Jubilant Daughter

MARCH 28, 2020

Dear Roberta,

Thanks to you, I have always had the ability to find a silver lining. While I may sarcastically call you "Positive Patty" during our conversations, I know deep down that I will always arrive at gratitude, no matter how long it takes to get there.

God chose me to be the proud Mom of three very different boys with autism; they are each on different levels of the spectrum and, like everyone, have their own unique strengths and abilities. Over the past few years, their differences have amplified the complexity of our household and even started to impact our ability to be in various community situations. I had been trying to keep a Band-Aid on this ever-growing issue while my gut was telling me that one day Andrew and I would need to make the dreaded residential placement decision to ensure that all three boys get the maximum amount of professional support during their school age years, and as you know, we waved the white flag last year when we embarked upon the journey to find the appropriate school for Michael.

One of our biggest challenges surrounding the "three factor" is their different sensory processing issues. Michael's hypersensitivity to different sounds includes screeching and certain tones of voice that make him uncomfortable, for example, overly monotone, rote, and electronic sounds or a high-pitched "Hooray." This, combined with Maxx's auditory sensory seeking tendencies such as vocalizations, high pitched giggling spells, and tapping objects, along with his use of an iPad to communicate and his ABA learning style that requires constant "hooray" reinforcement, means our family is primed for daily quarantine debacles.

The boys' different profiles on the spectrum have enabled me to identify with a bigger population of moms who have similar children although I haven't met as many moms who have children with Michael's profile as those with kids similar to Maxx and Dimitri. Often people think that he is a typical child with horrific behavior.

Remember the day that I called you, Mom, and we discussed Michael's new need to scream loudly, "shut up," at Maxx when he makes vocalizations in public? Then, there was the day that we went to a private autism-friendly movie viewing, and Andrew and I had to separate our family with a few seats in between because Michael was screaming "Shut up, I am trying to watch the movie" at Maxx. While I was slightly uncomfortable even in a private viewing, I never imagined in a million years that other autism moms were judging me, thinking that I had brought my autistic son's neurotypical sibling to a movie and that he was screaming at another child from another family in attendance and that I didn't walk over and apologize.

Wow, I remember the jarring Yahoo group thread with the subject of "Shut Up at Movie" that I found in my inbox after that weekend. The comments, like "Perhaps this Mom should consider hiring a behavior consultant," were beyond hurtful and laughable at the same time. Little did these Moms know that we do, indeed, have a village of behavior consultants parading in and out of our house all day long, and we were walking through the painful process of finding a therapeutic residential school for Michael. I know, Mom. I hear you saying in your quiet yet exacerbated tone, "Melanie, why in the world are you even letting something like this get you down? It was yesterday for Christ's sake. Let it go and do something for yourself today."

While only a few weeks into the quarantine, seeing the "three factor" even more amplified while locked down with each other solidifies our decision to send Michael to a residential school, at least for a year or two. He needs to be removed from our home for a period of time to have the professionals teach and counsel him twenty-four/seven on how he can enjoy life with us and utilize his ultra-technology savvy and other unique and employable skills.

I simply can't decide in my heart and my head what to be most heartbroken about, the actual day that we tell him about his new school or his soon-to-be absence from our home. Both days are dreaded by moms who walk through this circumstance when making the difficult decision to place their child in a therapeutic residential school. Some parents choose to tell their child prior to drop off day, but due to Michael's profile, that plan would not work for safety reasons during transport and for fear that he would run away before we leave. His new school decided to come to our house with staff who are complete strangers to him on pick up day, and Andrew and I have been advised to tell him only a few minutes before. That dreaded day was supposed to be on April 6th. How will I ever find the strength to get through this day or even imagine his absence after? The thoughts bring a flood of emotions, a river of tears, and shaking hands from panic. Now, that day will hang over my head for an indefinite period of time.

Love,

Mom at the Movies

MARCH 29, 2020

Dear Roberta,

Do you remember the day that I was so upset after Maxx's annual IEP meeting and the fact that we had to actually add a goal to teach him how to watch TV? His goal for that year was to watch TV for a five-minute period. He had absolutely no self-leisure skills whatsoever. Well Mom, he has risen to the occasion and has shown us in the past five days that he indeed knows how and enjoys watching TV for hours at a time! We are always so active on the weekends, and he is so busy after school that we never even realized it. What a gift from God at this time. Did you send that to me by chance?? I see you winking.

My anxiety is building about homeschooling, and I am super sensitive about the boys possibly not receiving the same quality of program that is being provided to the general education population. We moved to this district for their reputation for superior special education programs and services, and they have never let us down. Instead of feeling peace about these upcoming changes, I can't get these thoughts out of my head because it feels like an eternity until I can see what they have designed. It's tough to wait patiently as I have already seen two weekly suggestion packets disseminated to students who don't have profiles like my children, yet Dimitri and Michael have only received an email with a few documents and a suggested project. Maxx has received nothing. Every time that I see a text, email, or video update, my heart drops at the end because there is no mention of support for students like Maxx.

What's going to happen to Maxx during this pandemic? Are students with his profile going to be labeled as "not able to be educated during COVID-19" because they only maintain goals with face-to-face interaction? Is he going to be left to watch TV and stim around the house all day with a fidget toy? Mom, I am trying to keep my cool here — my relationships are everything to me, but remember, I did inherit your advocate hat as you had to advocate for my brother, Michael. I promise to keep my typing fingers quiet for a few more days.

Mom, do you remember the behavior consulting agency that I always raved about? We moved to this district to specifically have access to them as our district contracts with them to support students like Dimitri, Michael, and Maxx. Yes, Mom, I still miss my old home something fierce, but we are where we are for the boys. We moved here when Michael was in crisis, and I know in my heart and my gut that that the agency is going to rise yet again to be exactly what we need through the unknown of the next few weeks.

Maxx's parent trainer gave us another fabulous PowerPoint presentation on COVID-19, and it has helped tremendously with Dimitri. We keep reading it together over and over again, and it is helping him, although I see the anxiety building up in his eyes. I am trying to put together a homeschool routine, but wow, I am horrible at this, and I am sure that he sees right through me (LOL). I am trying to remember your guidance to always act "as if," even if you are unsure of yourself. Mom, I laugh when I think about you sitting in a corner watching me try to teach him with your face covered up by a book while snickering. I know that teaching is not my finest strength, OK? He is so disappointed right now, and I don't know how to make him happy. It's only been a few days, and he misses school so much.

Dimitri asked to earn the North of the North DVD about six weeks ago, and he has earned it over and over again since then, yet I continued to forget to order it. He inherited Dad's patience, not yours (LOL). I decided today that he MUST get it, and I was determined to find it. I called Dimitri's personal aide, Nick, and asked him to search high and low for it on the internet because we don't have access to sites like Walmart or Target at home due to Michael. Nick saw one at Target a few towns over. DONE! I drove over, mask, gloves, and alcohol (as a sanitizer, not a drink 😊) all in hand. This was an "essential" Mom — it was essential for me to see Dimitri smile for the first time in days. The site was not up-to-date, and there was no North of the

North DVD there. I called Nick in tears, and he found one that could be ordered and sent the receipt to me. Mom, my heart was broken into pieces when I pulled into the driveway because Dimitri was waiting in the window thinking that I was bringing home his DVD. I had to walk in and tell him that the computers were wrong but that I was able to order it, and I showed him the confirmation. He simply said, "Sometimes things change, and that's OK."

I made it to our bedroom before breaking down into tears where I remained for a good cry for ten minutes. I really wanted to reach out to Donna because I knew that she would understand. She's such a good listener. I knew she wasn't available at that time, so the thoughts exited my mind quickly.

It was a hard day, but I ended it with making your meatloaf. Seeing your handwriting on the recipe card gave me comfort. I took some time to thank God at the end of the night for strength and feel hopeful for tomorrow. For a few seconds, a very vivid picture of you entered my mind. I am so grateful that the liquor stores are closed. That was a really smart decision, Governor Cuomo. Glad you listened to Roberta.

Love,

Emotionally Exhausted

Hi Roberta!

I woke up this morning feeling empowered, energetic, and ready to face the day. I have outlined my goals for the day: 1) Adhere to Dimitri's homeschool program schedule so that he doesn't feel so anxious, 2) Prepare menus for the rest of the week, 3) Spend 30 minutes twice with Maxx on the computer doing puzzles, and 4) Wipe down the wall-sized whiteboard and organize it into sections for homeschool. I feel good. I've got this. I spritzed myself with your Estee Lauder Youth Dew to give me super Roberta strength, and I am barely thinking of Donna.

Michael woke up with a ton of anxiety — he saw a YouTube video made by a "friend" doing a "show" on the Wiggles CD albums that he got in the mail. Remember, he does not have access to online ordering, so his anxiety was through the roof on how he was going to get these items and how I could confirm that they were indeed purchased. He had his morning meds at 11:30 after he woke up at 11:15. By 2:00, I had dispensed his maximum daily dose of emergency medication. Oh God, I had seven more hours until he would go to sleep. Before 5:00, there had been multiple meltdowns with me trying to show him that I was trying to purchase it. At 5:00 on the dot, we had to leave the house to go outside of our WiFi area and drive around the corner so that he was able to see the merchandise he wanted. Damn it! Now I taught him again that if he has meltdowns, he gets what he wants. I had to do it to keep everyone safe in our house.

The day that would never end got even better when something happened to Dimitri's Instagram account. The app was requesting a password that I couldn't remember, and neither could he. Instagram is his world and his way to connect to his "teenager friends." His anxiety was increasing as he saw that I couldn't remember the password.

At 6:00, the shit hit the fan, and I just couldn't take it anymore. Michael's constant badgering and interruptions were just more than I could handle. I snapped and yelled at him. Now, the shit would really hit the fan since once I scream at him, it gets worse (remember he screams "shut up" and "F!@# you" all the time to me). Dimitri snapped and there was a brawl. Michael broke a plate, and Dimitri was headed towards the TV, his favorite thing to break when he is frustrated. He made it past me and punched it three times. Andrew was trying to hold him back, but Dimitri ran into the refrigerator to grab two cartons of eggs and proceeded to throw them all at the TV to ensure that he had indeed finished the mission.

Michael then came in calmly and said that he had called the police because there was an argument. We were trying to clean everything up so that no one got hurt, and it dawned on me that Maxx was nowhere to be found. Mom, I found him hiding in the bathroom. He was half laughing because he wasn't sure if the aggression in our family was supposed to be funny or scary. I quickly locked the door and hugged him as tightly as I could. I shouted out at Andrew and asked for pants and sneakers as I knew that I had to get him out of the house to keep him safe and then scramble to get a new TV.

The police arrived as I was leaving — they were so kind, and I so wanted to hug the two policewomen. I met Nick at Target so that he could watch Maxx as I went inside. It was closed — today was their first day closing early. I stood outside the store crying and begging the manager to let me purchase a TV while promising to be in and out in less than two minutes. I even handed him my card and told him to pick it out and that I didn't care how much it was. He wouldn't let me! I lost it and was shouting at him, "I spend over $1,000 a month here and am practically here every day — as a matter of fact, I was just here this morning and spent $175." He couldn't have cared less Mom. I then heard Nick shout "Walmart! Walmart! They are still open!" We scrambled there as fast as we could. I ran in and grabbed the first TV that I saw — thank God it was on sale for $278. Time in and out — less than seven minutes. On my way out, I caved and called a friend to get wine. I need "out" right now, and alcohol is the fastest route. Fortunately, she only had red wine or hard liquor, neither that I like nearly as much as Donna, so I decided to go home with only a new TV.

So much for goals. There is always tomorrow.

Love,

Diving for the Touchdown

APRIL 1, 2020

Dear Roberta,

Your teddy bear, Dimitri, is clearly depressed, and I feel helpless. I know that he is very anxious to see what his homeschool schedule looks like, and I am trying to deliver a half-ass program that I put together during the time that I would normally be sleeping. I am trying so badly to help him. He wants a written schedule with classes and 100% of my attention like the teachers give. He likes the apps that I purchased and loves checking off his schedule, but it is only for an hour, and during that time, I am being continuously interrupted by Maxx and Michael and getting pulled in what seems like 100 different directions. He is patient, but I can see the disappointment on his face. Every night, when I put him to bed, he says, "Excuse me Mom, we didn't do . . . (things like social studies, his bank balance sheet, physical education)." I always walk out of his bedroom with a heavy heart.

This feeling that I didn't do enough is all new to me as you know, Mom. I pride myself in making sacrifices that enable us to provide every opportunity that I think would help my children succeed, despite their disabilities. Feeling defeat in this area of my life is very uncomfortable and downright depressing. I am helpless, and it is out of my control. God grant me the serenity to accept the things that I cannot change . . .

I have to break it to him that Easter is not happening, at least not what he is used to with his cousins whom he adores being with. I am just dreading it. It seems like the annual Easter gathering is the only thing that is keeping him going right now. You know how much he loves holidays! He practically lives for them and starts planning and decorating for the next one before the closest upcoming one isn't even finished. I swear the kid should work at Hallmark one day.

I know the question that's coming after I tell him that we are not observing Easter the way that we usually do at church. Like everyone else, we are so saddened that we will miss the celebration at midnight on Holy Saturday with lit candles from his godparents, the parade around the church, and the Greek feast with family on Easter Sunday, including a roasted lamb in the backyard. I will do my best to buy tsoureki, traditional Greek bread with red eggs, and prepare the meal at home. Still, a flood of questions is to be expected about Memorial Day and will most likely be followed by July the 4th in the same conversation.

Love,

Holding Out for a Holiday

Dear Roberta,

I often wonder if other parents have the same time management challenges that I do right now. I see them on social media making comments about the "homeschool drag," but the difference that I don't ever see being brought to light is that ASD Moms almost always have to be sitting beside their students for all learning activities, and at times, in the case of Maxx for example, it is 100% hand over hand repeating every single word that the teacher says.

My phone and email are blowing up from professionals to schedule virtual programs, but for the love of God, I am only one person, Mom! This is the challenge that I face right now, all in the tiny three-bedroom house that we live in. I feel like one of those bendy dolls being pulled and twisted in every single position I can because I have to be with them during all of their virtual sessions, with the exception of Michael for two half-hour slots each day.

I think that yesterday was Wednesday. I have an open slot on Monday and Thursday, so moving someone's therapy to another day would be helpful as Wednesdays certainly are not my favorite day of the week.

5:30 A.M.
BLEEPING ALARM GOES OFF . . . TIME TO GET UP AND AT IT.

I wake up, nurse a cooling pot of coffee and prep multiple meals for three different and limited food repertoires. The printer spits out the schedules and support documents the boys and I need for the day. By the time I update the whiteboard schedule and begin checking email, Maxx is starting to stir.

6:30 A.M.
HELLO SUNSHINE! MAXX IS UP.

Maxx wakes up. I guide him through all of his daily living skills including toileting, hand washing, dressing, etc. We practice brushing our teeth together for as long as he can stand it. While he watches Blue's Clues, I prepare food and drinks for the boys, making sure to add the correct supplements and medications — all the while keeping noise to a minimum so that the twins can sleep. I try not to watch Governor Cuomo's or Mayor DeBlasio's morning briefings, but I do take a quick look on the special needs Facebook groups to get updates on classes available that perhaps may be useful for Dimitri. (The classes are never a good fit for Maxx or Michael.)

9:00 A.M. — 12:00 P.M.
JUGGLING 101 BEGINS.

Juggle Dimitri's art and music class while managing the noise so that he can participate and enjoy the classes. I have to keep an eye on Maxx continuously as he often runs into the "cubby" while Dimitri is in class. I continuously answer questions from Michael and give in to his demands to keep the peace.

Midway through the morning, I set Michael and Maxx up on separate computers for their classes and juggle between the two of them. I do my best to manage Maxx's noises during his classes and keep his device voice low for fear that Michael might break away from his class and throw toys at us. Michael's laptop is super slow lately so some days all three boys have to use the same desktop computer in the living room for schoolwork, which leaves one of them missing a class or two. Wow, I wish I just had the time to make that phone call to arrange having his laptop serviced.

12:00 — 1:00 P.M.
JUGGLING 102

Serve the three different lunches and snacks I prepped this morning while keeping peace in the household. I practice eating at the table with Maxx again and answer a slew of questions. Clean up.

1:00 — 3:30 P.M.
MASTER OF JUGGLING 103

Set Dimitri up for his favorite Suffolk JCC-Y virtual class: Theater. Oh, how Dimitri loves theater! Mom, you would love to hear him participate. This class brings me so much joy, even though I have to juggle listening to him, keeping the noise down, and keeping his "class area" private to avoid Maxx walking in with only his underwear on. The Y has been such an indispensable part of Dimitri's homeschool program with their invaluable enrichment programs. I honestly don't know what I would do without them right now!

After theater, it's time for Maxx's occupational therapy appointment. Wow! He makes a lot of noise during the sessions as he alternates between joy and resistance to requests. Even though he smiles when he sees his OT teacher, he still runs away from the "cubby" a lot. It's a perfect time for Maxx to practice using his device and asking for what he wants, but I need to be mindful of possible toys flying through the air at us or toward the computer screen.

By this time of the day, Dimitri is done with the various noises and protests. His patience is at its limits. I always make sure to give him positive praise for practicing his breathing exercises and affirm when he uses his coping mechanism of staying downstairs out of the chaos.

3:30 — 5:30 P.M.
FREE TIME FOR ALL, EXCEPT ME AND ANDREW

Every day at this time, I can tell that Maxx needs to get out, so I take him on a 45-minute drive. This is a necessary soothing time for him as he listens to music and enjoys the ride. I do my best to make this time interruption-free, but sometimes, I have to use this time to return calls to teachers and therapists.

Andrew has to bring his workstation upstairs while I am out of the house because the microwave in our kitchen (also upstairs) has to be watched at all times for fear that Michael may microwave a non-edible item.

When we get home, I start dinner or make a quick run for essentials. Michael has his virtual instruction time with Ms. Cari soon afterward, so I set his computer up along with what he needs for daily hygiene skills such as showering and toothbrushing. He refuses to perform these skills if I tell him; he will only do it if Ms. Cari tells him to.

5:30 — 6:15 P.M.
MICHAEL'S VIRTUAL INSTRUCTION TIME — EXHALE

Mom, there are no words to describe the gratitude that I feel for Ms. Cari. She's been Michael's 1:1 behavior consultant throughout the school year and does Google classroom with him. During these 45 minutes, he's a rockstar, and she's one no-nonsense bad ass homeschool teacher.

6:15 — 8:00 P.M.
DINNERTIME

Serve up dinner to the twins, practice eating dinner at the table with Maxx, clean up dinner. Try not to watch Governor Cuomo's or Mayor DeBlasio's evening briefings.

8:00 — 9:00 P.M.
WINDING DOWN FOR BEDTIME

Give Maxx a shower and ensure that Dimitri takes one. Dimitri is so good, Mom; I rarely have to remind him to shower. Thank God for this easy child. After the showers, Andrew and I give Dimitri and Maxx their medication. It's also around the time I give Michael his "bedtime snack," vanilla yogurt with cookie crumbs discreetly laced with his Risperdal and Clonidine, antipsychotic medications.

After the whirlwind evening routine, I crash while Andrew, the god of patience, stays up for another two hours to finish any office work and help with household needs. He has turned into my daily tag-team partner who also sleeps in my bed. I try so hard not to interrupt him while he is working, but there are times, of course, when I just can't manage doing four things at once. I wonder if he secretly cringes every time I call his name.

One of the biggest changes that I have made during the pandemic is to head right to bed after we put the boys to bed. I am in bed no later than 9:45 p.m. Pre-pandemic, this would have been my time with Donna.

Thoughts of my non-Donna friends go through my head throughout the day as I barely have the time to type "thinking of you." I try to find a second to call to hear their voices, but it's usually at a time when they can't speak, like with my friend Karen, a first responder nurse who works at a drive-through, testing potential COVID-19 patients. I miss her so much. I also feel horrible for not being a visible support to my friend, Elisa, who recently lost her Mom to COVID-19. Rarely a day went by before the pandemic that we didn't speak or email, but now, we have only connected twice since quarantine, and even then, it was only for a few minutes.

The only people that I get to speak to for longer than five minutes other than Andrew are the indispensable behavior consultants who call every day for Michael. Sometimes, I think how much I am going to miss them too when Michael moves to Boston. How can I just abruptly stop talking to someone that I have spoken to every single day during the initial quarantine of a pandemic? It's such a vulnerable period, and the bonds that you make during this time are stronger and deeper than normal.

Andrew and I just shake our heads every time that we see the lockdown referred to as "downtime" on TV.

Tomorrow, the alarm goes off at 5:30 a.m., and we'll hit the ground running again.

Love,

Sleepless in Long Island

APRIL 6, 2020

Dear Roberta,

You know that I love these children dearly, but COME ON . . . do you really think that even YOU would be able to manage answering nonstop questions all day and evening, and even at night if they are up, without going completely out of your mind at times? I still remember your beautiful face all dolled up with pink lipstick giggling to yourself when the boys were driving me crazy as toddlers. I would shout, "It's not funny!" like I did as a teenager, and we would laugh hysterically. There are also memories of us sitting at your kitchen table drinking coffee in the morning, having serious conversations and you just shaking your head, never letting a mean word escape your lips.

Dimitri, whose extreme OCD makes him anxious about schedules, has now magically adjusted to the concept of no school. I seriously can't believe that he just accepted it like that. It was one of my biggest concerns at the beginning of the quarantine, but he magically doesn't ask when he is going back. He does, however, often ask the question, "What do you think about COVID?" during virtual sessions and to anyone other than myself or Andrew.

I have been taught by the behavior consultants to tell the boys that I will answer the same question only two to three times a day, and after that, I will point to the schedule or pre-printed answers. That plan was great pre-quarantine, but now, I don't even have time to write down the questions or answers on the massive blackboard walls painted in my kitchen.

Mom, anyone would send a thousand "I've got nothing" memes today after reading this sample of random questions and explanations over the past few days:

DIMITRI:

Excuse me Mom, what time does breakfast start? What time does it end? What time will you start making it? What day, time, and where did you buy the ingredients?

What time will the trash truck come today? Yesterday it came at 10:52 not 10:50.

Mom's going out for essentials today? Where? What route will you take? What time will you leave? What time will you leave there? What time will you be home? He checks the receipts when I get home to make sure when I left to reconcile with when I got home.

What time does homeschool start today? What time will it end? He is sitting in his seat five minutes prior to the time and starts watching my every move if I am late. I continue to tell him that homeschool is flexible, but flexibility is not one of his better qualities . . . we are working on that.

Will Zoom work properly at dance class today? It made the class two minutes late yesterday. Zoom's not going to be late again today, right?

Does the mail run today? I know that he wants to ask me if he will be late, but he is holding himself back after I give him the "don't-even-ask-me-about-the-time" look (LOL).

Where are we going on our long drive today? What time are we leaving? Mom's going to get Maxx's clothes on at what time? What route are we taking? We will be at Exit 64 at what time?

What day is my playbill coming? Dimitri can order another one when? He knows that he can only order items by earning money on his balance sheet by doing chores.

Excuse me Mom, what time does Maxx have homeschool today? He doesn't ask about Michael because Michael only participates two times a day with his behavior consultant, 11:45 and 5:30. Those times are very predictable, thank God.

Needless to say, Dimitri will NEVER be a NY minute late for a job when he gets older. Punctual is not even a good description.

MICHAEL:

Do you remember that day during Storm Sandy when Ashton Kutcher wore the same bow tie as Peppa Pig's parents?

Do you know what day is Jeff Fatt's (purple Wiggle) mom's birthday?

Whose name is wrong in the Pop Go the Wiggles US CD version song credits? — it's only in the US CD version. Someone's name is wrong in the song credits.

Do the Sprout recordings of The Wiggles belong to the Australian Broadcasting Corporation? It sure would be nice if more Americans had copies of them.

Is there an error in the credits of Cold Spaghetti Western? The introduction tracks are not listed in the US version, only the Australian version.

Did the guest star on Racing to the Rainbow pass away after your Dad in 2008?

Are the Spanish versions of the Wiggles owned by the Australian Broadcast Company?

Do you remember the 2018 finale of the ABC Kids logo?

Which one is better? HIT Entertainment or Warner Home Video?

What day did the Wiggles come out in Tokyo?

What song credit is missing Marie Field's name on the US version of Yummy Yummy, but it's right on the Australian version?

What do Dr. Oz and Anthony Field have in common? Yep — they wear the same ring. Mom, I always wondered why he became so interested in Dr. Oz last year, and then when he finally told me, Andrew and I were dying laughing. I should have known that everything in his head circles back to the Wiggles somehow. I had to take a look myself, and yes, the rings look alike (LOL). He even found a way to get us seats at the Dr. Oz show independently. I was surprised to receive a call confirming our attendance a few days before. Good times!

What day did Brian Mohler and Lori Bernstein leave the Laurie Berkner band? Yep, the same day that Greg Page left The Wiggles.

Will it flush the M&M's? He gets this from a YouTube show that he just started watching where people flush random things down the toilet. UGH! I answer, "No, that's not a good idea." Then he answers, "They use the peanut M&M's." This conversation exchange happens at least twenty times a day, and even Maxx, who is nonverbal, is trying to say the end of the sentence with him, "use the peanut M&M's." I will make sure to mention the food flushing show to the staff at his new school.

Is it OK to flush a grilled cheese sandwich?

Is it OK to microwave a Christmas decoration? Another brilliant idea that he conceived after watching a YouTube show with a ridiculous number of followers who watch young men microwave non-edible items. Yep . . . added to "the list" for the school.

Why don't you like the video with the pet tiger?

He knows the answers to all of the questions, and when I guess he says, "Actually, . . ." and gives the answer. These questions are asked repetitively throughout each day, and he laughs at the funny ones because he knows that he is being silly.

Love,

Questioned OUT

APRIL 7, 2020

Dear Roberta,

While I know that you didn't order things online personally before you went to your new glorious home, I know that you understood the importance and convenience of it. These days, ordering things online is an everyday event in most homes, as routine as eating or showering. Of course, our home has to be different, but the technology gymnastics we go through in order to keep Michael from fixating on new items has created an exponential inconvenience during the pandemic.

As you know, Michael's anxiety challenges surround having access to every single version of anything that is in his "preferred list of items" in his brain at the time. This exercise could require me to go to great lengths to find an item such as a DVD with a "Great Buy" sticker that he may have seen a friend "unbox" on YouTube, or a Wiggles birthday cake candle with slightly different packaging. Once he gets it in his head that he has to have this item, he will hold us hostage until he gets it, using tactics including refusing to take the bus, running down the street if we are going somewhere, damaging property, or winding himself up into a full on panic attack that requires the police to come and either a) make him take his medicine and stay until he calms down or b) take him to the hospital for a psychiatric evaluation, which always ends with him being discharged hours later.

Due to his needs and after several hospitalizations, we were forced to have complex servers designed and installed into our home with multiple layers of technology security that block access to any site that has online ordering capabilities. Sometimes, he still gets through the firewalls, and we have to make adjustments, but overall, it helps manage his "item anxiety." Ten years ago, this may not have been such a big deal, but for the love of God, we are in a global pandemic, and we need to order essentials!

Mom, I have often thought about how much I would have loved for you to meet Nick and Christian, the twenty-four-year-old twins that live in our town who have worked for us for six years! Remember, I told you about COMHAB? In New York, it stands for Community Habilitation Workers. I love them as my own, and I know that you would have loved them as your own as well. I miss them so much during this time.

One cannot live without millennials during a pandemic! They have been my lifesavers before, but now, wow! We have developed quite a process. Remember, I can't even google anything that can be ordered, so I simply text them the search engine Boolean, and within a military second, I get pictures of items. I trust them as I would trust you, and they have meticulous lists of information in their brains to know how to order items that we need.

Yesterday, I remembered that I brought home a few of your night gowns when we were cleaning your house out with intentions of making them into a blanket. I am so glad that I didn't. They have been sitting in the duffle bag beside my bed where I dropped them when I came home from the funeral. I got them out before I went to bed. They were perfectly folded as if you folded them yesterday. I also brought home two of your blouses to use in the blanket, and I smiled as I could see you wearing them with your pink lipstick.

I am so enjoying my night-time prayers and meditation before I go to sleep every night. I thanked God for giving me sobriety again, but I can't even remember how many days it has been. The last time I was sober, I had been counting the seconds.

Love,

Online Ordering is OUT

APRIL 8, 2020

Dear Roberta,

What day is it? I have no idea but it's now 10:00 a.m., and I can see that the day is going south very quickly. Michael is perseverating on some CD cases that he saw on the internet. He likes to have blank ones — not sure why. The ones that he saw are different in that they have two staples in the binding unlike the ones that he has now with three. I didn't see them ordered in my email and asked Christian if he ordered them. He said that he couldn't find them. PANIC.

Michael suddenly remembered that he had somehow seen them at Target, but I don't think that he had. I knew that he was making it up so that he could go inside the store and purchase every single DVD that he can find. There is no way that I can risk our family's lives to take him there, not to mention the cost factor. He hasn't been inside a brick and mortar store for over a year. He was building up, shouting "shut up" frequently and demanding that I find him clothes to wear to go out. I was afraid that if he got outside of the door he would run to Target, about a mile away from our house. I was able to give him meds and quickly exit the house, saying that I was going to get my medicine and would be back shortly.

I got in the van and start driving. Think outside the box, I told myself. I quickly called Ms. Cari, his daily behavior consultant, and asked her to create a sign indicating that children under the age of eighteen are not allowed in Target due to the coronavirus pandemic. She designed it perfectly, starting with "Dear Customers," ending with "Thank You for Your Patronage," and even adding a Target logo. He bought it — sigh of relief. I told him that I went there to see if they had the CD cases with two staples and saw that sign on the door. He said he would just purchase it on eBay. Nick later found the cases online, so I showed him the screenshot that it was ordered, and his mood changed instantly.

I spent two hours working in the front yard reseeding. The neighbor and his three children were outside. I went inside to get the sidewalk chalk and asked Dimitri if he wanted to come outside and help me decorate the street. The neighbor's kids also helped. Another neighbor came out, and we decorated the street with positive quotes and pictures of rainbows. We all laughed at the idea of when else would we all come out as neighbors and decorate the street with chalk? My favorite message was the one that said, "Hope Doesn't Cancel."

After showers and medication, I ended the day watching the country music concert. It was the first time that I sat down and watched TV without having Donna sitting on the windowsill behind me. How many days has it been anyway? I can't even remember.

I fell asleep feeling uplifted. Maxx woke up at 1:30, went back to sleep at 2:00, and slept through the rest of the night for the first time since quarantine.

Love,

Donna-less Daughter

Dear Roberta,

Today is Maxx's birthday and I know that the first call would have been from you singing "Happy Birthday" to him. As usual I would have thanked you and had a short conversation with you to begin the day without you knowing that tears were streaming down my face. Birthdays can be bittersweet in the autism world and often painful for ASD Moms. Another year of achievements, yet another year of your child being far behind everyone else their age. It's pouring outside, but I went to the bakery to pick up his cake, and I don't have any balloons or presents. I wonder what's happening with the order for his adult tricycle; he could really use it right now. I see the other kids riding their bikes up and down our street every day, and I long for him to be included. It would make his little life that has been even further reduced by COVID so happy. Damn you autism!

A good friend posted his birthday on Facebook in the local moms' group, and so many have wished him Happy Birthday. Trying to keep positive, but the tears are starting to happen every other minute. It just occurred to me that it's only 11:44 a.m. and the liquor stores are still open.

I went outside to start the reseeding process for the front yard in the pouring rain. It's easier to rake when the ground is wet. All of a sudden, I heard a horn, and a family came by to wish Maxx a happy birthday. They decorated their car so beautifully. Maxx was buckling over from giggling. Such kindness.

Later in the day, we tried teletherapy with one of Maxx's program instructors. After thinking about this for the past few months, I suddenly decided that now, during a global pandemic, was the time to have a heart-to-heart conversation and communicate that the current approach in this "puzzle piece" of his program wasn't working. I kept scratching my head wondering why I had been so reluctant to speak up before the pandemic, but nevertheless, it was time. This instruction is critical in order for him to communicate. The end result was unfortunate, the instructor resigned from his case because we didn't agree on the program that I think Maxx needs.

Initially, I panicked after the conversation, and then I reminded myself — my gut has been and is always right. My son, my decision. Maxx is twelve years old and nonverbal, so time is not on our side (especially in the quarantine), and he relies on me to make the right decisions surrounding his learning. I've got this! He will begin the program that I think is best immediately, even if it's during a pandemic when we only have virtual capabilities. Technology needs to be changed, a program needs to be written, and the village of people on his treatment team need to get on the same page to make this happen. Chop Chop! Let's get going. I feel invigorated and excited to see him soar.

It just dawned on me that we are well into April, Autism Awareness Month. Usually, I have blue ribbons, signs, and lights decorating my home, but not this year. Believe me, Mom, I am very well aware of autism.

Love,

Aware of the Kindness

APRIL 21, 2020

Dear Roberta,

Oh boy, do I have a laughable problem that I am sure many parents would dream to have. Dimitri cannot stop doing chores. The more chores the better, and the number of chores done per day has to be ever-increasing. I can only imagine your silence and then chuckling on the other end of the phone if we were speaking. You would get it of course and read my mind before I told you the details.

Before COVID-19 he had been learning about a bank account at school. He was also working at a local restaurant putting together to-go boxes one day a week, and I told him that he would earn five dollars for every day that he worked. I opened a bank account up for him and the plan was for him to learn how to deposit his five dollars and learn the value of money and purchasing Broadway playbills that he collects. This was right before the pandemic, so we only got as far as opening the account.

The school sent home the suggestion to create a bank balance sheet and teach your child how to do chores, which honestly, I should have done a long time ago but never had enough time. A few weeks ago, I created the balance sheet in Google Docs and WOW! Not only is he teaching himself the app which, by the way, my husband doesn't even know anything about, but he is on fire with doing chores. That's a good thing, right?

Seeing the numbers get higher on the balance sheet is so motivating to him! While he only earns thirty cents per chore, I find myself telling him to stop doing chores multiple times a day, sometimes with a very stern voice. I even saw on his computer that he was googling how to do chores. Yesterday, his balance sheet had washing the dishes five times, unloading the dishwasher, turning on the dishwasher, unpacking the groceries, throwing out the garbage seven times, wiping down the counters five times, sweeping the crumbs three times, cleaning the inside of the vacuum cleaner, cleaning the outside of the steam mop, dusting the furniture three times, cleaning up various "Maxx food messes," planting grass seeds, raking the mulch two times, and sweeping the sidewalks. I finally had to tell him at 8:30 p.m. that there was to be no more talking about chores today. Then before bed, he said, "I can't wait to do chores again tomorrow." As I was walking out of his bedroom, I heard him whisper, "I am looking forward to cleaning the windows tomorrow."

He has to be supervised somewhat while doing these chores because he uses too many paper towels and too much cleaning solution. Speaking of cleaning solution, he became very upset when I didn't purchase the same brands that we have had from the past two weeks. He takes the initiative to do chores without our supervision, like by cleaning the inside of my new Shark vacuum, which left us missing a few pieces when we had to put back together.

While this is incredibly helpful, I can see the drive in his eyes and can see how this could turn into a very serious OCD situation very quickly. I need to use this time at home to capitalize on this need for ever increasing numbers. Hmmmm.

Love,

Mom With a Plan

Dear Roberta,

I am super sensitive these days, and the drive-by birthday parties in my neighborhood are really starting to get to me. My friendships with moms who don't have children with disabilities are dear to my heart, and your coaching has been indispensable. COVID-19 tries every ounce of empathy I have left. It feels so much worse having to struggle more than my neighbors seem to. The isolation is even more challenging for families like ours.

I am barely getting by, minute by minute, and seeing the multitude of students with signs driving by to say Happy Birthday brings that familiar "sting" to my heart for a second. Yes, I know, Mom; I don't know what happens in their house, and they may suffer from some challenges of their own. What I do know is that these children have a lot of friends who can speak and draw signs and some who can even drive a car, and I know that Maxx only had one drive-by for his recent birthday. It just reminds me of that meme that says, "we are not all in the same boat during quarantine." I would give the world for my children to have that many friends.

For a NY minute, I realized that today is Saturday, and I took a moment to remember what Saturdays used to look like for us pre-COVID. Quite often, we had an autism-friendly community event sponsored by my favorite Long Island charity, Nassau Suffolk Autism Society of America. I love those ladies so much — they really work their rear ends off to provide private events for families like ours to attend in places that we couldn't usually visit, like amusement parks, private movies, and theater performances. Their events are beyond priceless to us. Afterwards, we would usually go out to lunch at Patrizia's Pizzeria, in Commack, a well-known restaurant that treats our family like royalty every week. I miss every single member of their staff terribly.

I find solace in friends who, like me, have a child with ASD. Mom, I would give anything for you to meet my good friend Keri, who has a fifteen-year-old child on the spectrum who "works for produce" on his behavior plan. If he earns all of his "good behavior checks," he earns the purchase of nineteen pieces of produce three days a week. He then moves on to eat all nineteen pieces of produce on the same day, knows every sku number for produce at the local market, and knows trivia about specific days going back years ago when produce was sold out or not in season. Both he and Dimitri share similarly specific bedtimes — Dimitri goes to bed at 9:09 and Keri's son goes to bed at 10:11.

Keri and I are also so much alike and find ourselves howling sometimes when we're on the phone. I do adore her so much, and I know that you would as well.

Yesterday, I got really lucky and had the time to connect with my new friend Sonya, whom I am leaning on for support through Michael's transition to residential school. Her daughter, Emily, fourteen, was placed at an out-of-state residential school two years ago after all attempts to resolve her physical aggression and self-injurious behavior were exhausted. Emily has made tremendous progress, and Sonya usually sees her every other weekend, but now due to the quarantine, Sonya hasn't seen her in over two months. I can't even imagine how she is making it through the days, and to top it off, all of the children in Emily's residential home contracted COVID-19 in addition to two house support staff members. Thank God, there have been minimal symptoms, but Sonya is on pins and needles until she can bring Emily home for a weekend.

I have tried to connect with my friend Barbara, who has three boys in residential school homes on Long Island, but unfortunately, we have been playing phone tag. She is a nurse and is incredibly strong, but I can't even imagine how she is getting through the days right now.

Before I sign off, I have to tell you quickly that I found out Maxx's tricycle was declared lost. The store not only cancelled the order after seven weeks, but they said that they do not expect any more in. Wow. Can't he just get a break sometimes? The thought of giving Maxx his tricycle and watching him ride on the streets with the other children was keeping me going. I felt like this one thing would bring some happiness to him right now. I am devastated, Mom.

Love,

Entitled to my Pity Party

MAY 10, 2020

Dear Roberta,

Happy Mother's Day! I wonder what Mother's Day is like where you are, and something is telling me that it's nothing like the church Mother-Daughter banquets that we used to attend every year. I miss you, Mom. Things really haven't been the same since you passed.

How do they celebrate Mother's Day in Heaven? I imagine harps playing outside of each mansion with pink flowers galore and the angels . . . oh the angels.

Today, I received a special Mother's Day quarantine gift. We were invited to participate in a surprise recognition for our priests, Fr. Christopher and Fr. Constantin, who now celebrate the Sunday morning liturgy in our church alone, a church that was once packed with parishioners. Imagine their surprise when they walked out of the back of the church after liturgy to a parking lot with honking horns, cowbells, and vehicles with messages of gratitude written on their windows. When they walked out, a sense of comfort came over me unlike any other time during the quarantine. We were able to drive by and give a personal, socially distanced thank you, and I know that they are praying for our family.

While it was comforting to be in the parking lot, I couldn't help but look around at the parking lot's emptiness, despite the cars, as our annual Greek festival and so many other celebrations and events that take place here are now cancelled. Oh yes, the Greek festival, a tradition for parishes around the world that brings communities together to celebrate our heritage and our faith. My thoughts go to my father-in-law, who has worked tirelessly for over twenty years to support the event and how disappointed he is that it is cancelled. He takes such pride in giving the parish tours and explaining the history. He is well known at the church for welcoming everyone when they enter, distributing the church bulletins, and fostering English as the first language during liturgies. We are all so worried about him after his fall in March requiring multiple surgeries and an inpatient rehabilitation stay at a facility near our house. We haven't seen him once since we received the call from the hospital, due to COVID-19 visitation restrictions. The best that we can do is participate in daily Zoom calls when he is up to it, speak to his treatment team on a regular basis, and pray continuously for his safety during recovery.

Our parish has lost around fifteen parishioners, many with very visible volunteer roles in the church and even a couple in their fifties with school-aged children. For some reason, my mind went to us sitting on your front deck swing in the early morning drinking coffee together and how we could have a conversation about how pandemics shouldn't be allowed to touch houses of worship. It just doesn't seem logical; a church should be in a holy bubble with the anti-microbial properties of a gallon of hand sanitizer.

On the drive home, I thought about how I long to be inside the pristine walls of the Greek Orthodox Cathedral of St. Paul. I dreamt about what it will be like to walk in again and see the splendor of the architecture and iconography that makes me feel like I've stepped into a sliver of heaven. What I would have given to see and feel just a second of the reverence, awe, and glory to God that it demands upon entrance today. I would feel so lucky, Mom, to sit in a pew to pray in front of the large icon of Jesus Christ on the high wall behind the altar. I wondered how the priests will manage physical church attendance during NY's Phase 1 "Pause" return? Perhaps a lottery?

Love,

Missing Mom and St. Paul's

MAY 14, 2020

Dear Roberta,

I remember when I used to take time to thank God for the day each night at bedtime and then have a few seconds to think about you, and I felt like we somehow connected even though you were gone. I miss that time, and as I write, I remember why it stopped.

Even though you suddenly left three years ago, I still have that random urge to call you and tell you something quite frequently. I have heard that the urge never goes away. I will never forget the call from my sister with the news that she found you after you hadn't shown up for your weekly hair appointment. I miss you so terribly.

Mom, I have to be honest and tell you that I have wondered where you have been the past three years. I somehow thought that you would show me signs that you are still around in spirit. I have needed you so much over these past few years and can't help but feel abandoned. I do believe in contact from those who have passed on, and I keep waiting for you.

Last year, I hosted a fundraiser for Camp Loyaltown, the boys' sleep-away camp, and sponsored a psychic medium who specializes in contacting those who have gone to the other side. My heart was shattered that you didn't come through for me. I just keep holding on to the idea of somehow, someway hearing from you before we meet again.

I am so jealous of the moms in my network who have mothers who are still alive. I remember you constantly telling me that God certainly had a plan when he picked me to be Dimitri, Michael, and Maxx's mom. Well, I know that he had a plan when he picked you to be my mom because you coached me to be strong, courageous, and a constant advocate for my children. I do hope that you heard everyone who spoke at your funeral — the word strong was used consistently over and over again. The word charitable was also used since you left a legacy of supporting those in need.

Well Roberta, . . . it appears that I am in need right now, much more than you would have ever imagined when you were alive.

Love,

Missed Connection with Mom

MAY 19, 2020

Dear Roberta,

Today is my and Andrew's 19th wedding anniversary. Wow. I honestly don't know how we made it this far, but here we are. Statistically, there is a high rate of divorce for parents of a child with autism. "A child." We have three and somehow have made it thus far.

I think back to our wedding day. We had purchased our first home in an affluent village on Long Island and had dreams of raising our children there, watching them play soccer in the popular soccer field that we drove by every day and seeing them follow their dreams.

Mom, I can't remember if we ever discussed the poem "Welcome to Holland." It's about a person who's making plans for a fabulous vacation in Italy, and then they surprisingly arrive in Holland instead. The poem goes on to describe how they soon begin to see the beauty of Holland and gifts that it offers, yet sometimes think back to Italy and wonder what their original vacation would have been like.

Speaking of vacations, our annual time away from the boys has been cancelled. Andrew and I get one week away from all three boys every year when they attend a magical camp in upstate NY, and it has been cancelled. It's the only time that we have as a couple — yes, I know, one time a year.

I started seeing a therapist before the pandemic, and she asked me how often Andrew and I have a meal alone together. My answer was once a year, then I corrected my answer to a few times a year but all within that one week when we are alone. The look of shock on her face was priceless. "You have an annual meal alone with your husband?" I tried to explain to her why, and she continued to be baffled.

We have to have support that can meet the needs of all three of our differently disabled children at one time, and that's tough. I realized in that session that the time I had been spending with my friend Donna helped fill the loneliness and need for time with Andrew. Together, the therapist and I decided that we were going to work together to find strategies to fix this problem, and then COVID laughed and laughed.

At least before the pandemic, Andrew and I had time to talk. We had very brief conversations during his commute to work or while he was in his office, and that was enough to move our household along more efficiently. I at least had time to brief him with necessary information about the boys, and even had time to talk about myself sometimes, and he did as well. That communication at least got us caught up enough to have a little husband and wife time on the weekends without starting from the beginning. Now, there is little or no communication between us whatsoever other than the times I suddenly find myself "sinking" in the homeschool schedule because I am overbooked and turn to him for help, despite the fact that he is still working one hundred percent, but now in a new virtual environment. Even when I do have a moment to start talking about something, I get pulled in another direction, and I just give up.

It's just the two of us, and we have to get it done somehow, so we are doing that as a team. There is no time for chit chat, even on the weekends, when we still have to find ways to fill their days without the usual entertaining diversions like autism friendly movies, family meals at restaurants, parties, church, etc. We both wake up every day at 5:30, even on the weekends, to catch up on outstanding housework, errands for essential items, or even actual office work in Andrew's case. I go to bed early because I can't function during these demanding days without sleep, and he comes to bed some time later. We do manage to say "good morning" to each other, but that's about it. Even on our long Sunday drives as a family, I have to sit in the back seat now because Maxx's noises agitate Michael, and we are afraid for his safety. Every few minutes, we will shout something at each other over the music.

A pandemic is nothing that you would ever think about experiencing together as a couple, but here we are, on our nineteenth wedding anniversary, in the middle of the biggest one in seventy years. I am proud of us, Mom. I am proud of what we have accomplished thus far in eight weeks, and the memories will only make us stronger.

Love,

Cuddling in COVID

Dear Roberta,

I think it's Monday. Mondays used to be a time for me to finally focus on something that I have for myself: my career. Before COVID, I had a village of people that came into the house after school, and of course the boys were in school during the day, so I was able to somehow juggle their meetings with teachers and the never-ending list of emails and phone calls required to maintain their programs, along with a career that I love.

Mom, you know how much my career as an Executive Recruiter and Career Coach means to me. Before the twins were born, I had a very visible VP role at a recognizable global investment bank. I always envisioned being a working mom and demonstrating the important point that women can be just as successful as men in the workplace. You were always so good at coaching me to keep my professional and financial independence, and that's what I hope for my boys and my clients.

Do you remember when I went back to work after Maxx was born? That's when I started in my official role as a recruiter. I can't tell you how many times I played match-maker for internal jobs in my role as VP at the bank. It felt so good and brought me such a deep level of joy to see my coworker's happiness when it all worked out, so it was a natural progression to return with my sole focus on recruiting.

Mom, you would be so proud of the book, *On Her Way Back*, that I recently co-authored with my manager and very close friend, Elisa. The book was such a labor of love for us. It's a step-by-step guide with clear and concise information for women on how to return to their careers. We published right before the COVID outbreak, so we plan to relaunch again when the job market picks back up.

My role as a Career Coach and VP of Diversity Acquisition at Right Executive Search has allowed me to carve out a specialty in supporting women who are returning to the workplace after extended family leave, and I know that will be needed now more than ever. Right before the pandemic, my role was expanded to include not only women but also minority candidates and — you guessed it, Mom — candidates with disabilities! This put me right where I wanted to be with my career. I was energized and incredibly busy defining our new strategy to support all diverse candidates and then, Boom! Coronavirus. Ugh.

I inherited your need for and recognition of the joy of helping others and giving back to the community, Mom. I am so lucky that I get to experience this joy in my career as well as my personal life, except when we are in the middle of the worst pandemic in seventy years. Mondays would always bring a busy day with my answering work emails, making calls, and coordinating administrative projects to market the agency and, more recently, the book. Unfortunately, I have had to put my career on pause to keep our household afloat. I miss my professional career so much and dream of the day when I can also focus on my personal self, if only for a few minutes a day.

Speaking of focusing on myself, I have decided to become a redhead after COVID. Remember when you used to call me hot-headed and sassy? Well, I love Sharon Osborne's hair, so I plan to borrow that vibrant red color to debut in my new coiffure, but I am beginning to wonder if I am going to make it to the hair stylist's chair before the end of summer. It's a big change for me so I have to find a colorist that is not afraid to try a drastic transformation and has a waitlist shorter than an eternity. I can only imagine how hard it is going to be to get an appointment after all of Long Island has gone for months without a haircut.

I also started Weight Watchers® again, the eating plan you taught me from the age of ten. Remember the days when you and I went in privately behind a curtain while our weight was documented, and we checked off five veggies, three fruits, two grains, two fats, and eight glasses of water every day on our antiquated legal sized-paper checklist? Thank you Mom, for committing to a healthy lifestyle, accepting an imperfect adherence, and setting the example as a Lifetime Member during the last decade or so of your life. I really hope that you saw the parade of your WW friends that came to say goodbye at your funeral. I remember thinking how incredibly grateful I was for the fun, friendship, social opportunities, and health-filled camaraderie that they provided to you during the last few years of your life.

PS – Adored the man at your funeral that told me about how he drove you to WW meetings and your hair appointments and shared lunches with you at Bob Evans 😊.

In closing, Mom, please please please send some extra empowerment for me tomorrow as I have an important meeting about Michael's upcoming move. I will not cry. I will not cry.

Love,

*Making the Most out
of Mondays*

MAY 21, 2020

Dear Roberta,

This morning, I looked at the calendar — it has been over ten weeks since Maxx has been at school or even anywhere outside of our van. There are rumors that there will be no extended school-year summer services for Maxx's school. I'm still trying to be optimistic, but my gut is telling me that these rumors will come to fruition.

Yesterday, I signed a petition called "The Forgotten Children," supporting inclusion of appropriate, credentialed professionals in the Bill Gates committee created by Governor Cuomo on the "Reimagine Education" strategy. In his coronavirus response press conference on May 6th, he questioned our "old education model of everyone sitting in a classroom with the teacher in front." He wants technology to be in the forefront. Fabulous, but it seems that he may have forgotten about Applied Behavior Analysis, teaching principles used widely throughout schools to teach students like Maxx. ABA is one-to-one intensive intervention teaching with well documented, data driven benchmarks. Maxx, like thousands of other children in NY, cannot learn via virtual school.

I have given the virtual learning method a good try, but thirty minutes here and there via Zoom with me sitting beside him is not going to cut it, Mr. Governor. Mom, Maxx has regressed so much, and I am beyond panicked. The self-stimulatory behaviors and vocalizations that we were working to decrease have increased by one hundred percent. Routine self-care skills have declined tremendously, even toileting, at times. Speaking of toileting, his goal of using a public restroom has been thrown out the window for what appears like an eternity.

If you could pick the worst autistic behavior to have during the coronavirus, we have it of course! Last year, Maxx started this strange behavior of stretching his eyes with his fingers to look at things. It's most definitely a stimulatory behavior of some sort in that he gets enjoyment out of seeing things in a distorted way. We have been trying to take data on the behavior and develop a strategy to squash it for quite some time, but now, it is back and at the least appropriate time. One of the biggest tips for reducing the spread of coronavirus is to eliminate touching your face! Wow. I have even had strangers comment that he is touching his face when we are taking a walk in the neighborhood. I snapped at one of them and replied, "He has autism," hoping that that would end the conversation exchange, but then, they had to snap back at me, "It doesn't matter; he still should not be touching his face." It's true, he shouldn't. I wish it was easy for me to keep reminding him to stop touching his face. How will we be able to take him anywhere if this behavior isn't corrected?

I was also really looking forward to targeting showering after Michael goes to his new school in Boston. Remember when we talked about this over vacation, Mom? We still haven't been able to tackle this issue. Maxx is terrified of the shower head, along with any water that may build up in the bottom of the bathtub while showering. He doesn't seem to be able to process where the bottom of the bathtub is. In order to run the ABA showering program, I need one to two people in my home to keep him from sliding on the bathroom floor if he tries to escape, all while I, in my bathing suit, slowly demonstrate to him that the shower is OK. This entire process is guided by documented goals that are data-driven by his success.

Most of the goals in Maxx's Individualized Education Plan (IEP) require physical cue prompting. Switching from an education model to a strategy with technology at the forefront would require a parent to be with the student at all times during virtual learning. Governor, parents have jobs and need to pay bills.

Off topic, Mom, I have some fabulous news to share with you. Maxx finally got his adult tricycle!!! It's bright blue with a big emoji smile bell. We picked it up yesterday; I so wish that you could have seen his face when we showed it to him and seen him riding up and down our street. He giggles hysterically when he rides past the other kids in our neighborhood and rings his bell over and over again. My legs are so sore today from jogging beside him, a welcomed and much-needed pain during quarantine.

Love,

Taking the Win

MAY 23, 2020

Dear Roberta,

It poured rain all day today. Along with it came my tears. The bag containing the book of documents requiring my and Andrew's signatures has been tucked underneath my desk since January. I purposely hid them so that neither of the twins would see them and perhaps subconsciously so that I couldn't see them.

Step 1: Open.

Step 2: Cry.

Step 3: Cry some more.

Step 4: Get myself together to mask and glove up to begin shopping.

There is a battle in my brain about the process here. I have found it both comforting and annoying when those few people that I have shared this process with have said, "Well, he is seventeen and would have been going away to college anyway. Just think of it as college." I know that they are trying to help, but at the same time, I find it rather insensitive.

Mom, I know that you get it; it's just not the same. Together, you prepare for college with your child. Then you wait together, open the response letter together, cry together when it turns out to be a rejection, and then you celebrate together when the acceptance letter finally arrives. You celebrate with everyone on social media for National Decision Day. It's not the same when your child enters a residential program. It just isn't.

A son or daughter going to college can call and tell you if they need something or if someone is being unkind to them. Sending your child to college is a door to a new chapter of life. Most parents dream of them starting a career post-graduation or even finding their future spouse while at college. It's not the same. Instead, I am feeling this indescribable pain of accepting that I am no longer able to manage parenting my son at home. A son or daughter going to college understands that it is just that. They understand that their home is still home, and college is just school. That is a hard idea for a child with autism to accept and understand in the beginning, and those first few months until they understand are heart-wrenching because they think they have been abandoned and/or kicked out of their home.

My personal description of this process does not contain the word together nor celebration. I would describe it as lonely and isolating, with a glimmer of hope that sometimes peeks through the end of the tunnel for just a second. Even in 2020, there seems to still be a stigma about the fact that you have placed your child in a group home, so parents try to hide it, at least in the beginning. Eventually, some of the parents seem to open up but only to people who they can trust to be nonjudgmental. Now, even more so with the pandemic, I try to stay away from social media because my feed seems to be filled with bad news about COVID spreading like wildfire through group homes and about local leaders who are actively advocating to fill the need of basic PPE, which, according to them, was overlooked as a priority, in addition to posts by friends trying to secure visitation rights. I feel as if I would be condemned for sure if some of my network found out that I am actually dropping my son off while so many people that I know are advocating for the ability to bring their child home.

Mom, how I envision us together. I would hug you, we would cry together, and I'd tell you through my tears what a failure I feel like right now, just you and me, mother to daughter. You are the only person that could share this vulnerable moment with me; even Donna wouldn't love me through this conversation like you. I would tell you how I feel that I didn't do enough or hadn't been a good enough mother. The laments of self-loathing go on and on.

You would let me cry my eyes out and then say, "Mel, don't you know that your expectations of mothering may not be the same as God's? Who are you to define what makes you a good mother? You are, in fact, an exceptional mother for making the decision to set your grief aside and allow professionals to teach and enable him to be the capable young man that you know, deep down in your heart, he can be. You are giving him an opportunity that many young men may not ever receive, while giving the other two young men in your life time to bloom independently as well. Remember how I taught you to raise your hand in class if you need help? Indeed, you learned then, and now you are raising your hand in motherhood to do what's best for everyone in your family."

Love,

Nothing's the Same

Dear Roberta,

Yay! Finally, a bit of good news for me to share. We are finally getting a new van after previously hoping that the transmission in our old one was not going to go out during the pandemic. Dimitri was thrilled to help me clean out our old one of course. In the process, I found my bag full of lip treatments, including balms, serums, and sticks. It brought my thoughts back to how I would layer them while I was driving because my lips were cracked and peeling so badly from being burned by the alcohol consumption. Mom, I am so proud to tell you that I have well over sixty days under my belt! I seriously cannot believe it.

I try to have Hoda and Jenna on in the background in the living room and turn the volume up between home-school sessions when I see something interesting. Today, I saw the headline, "How I am Leaving the Pandemic," come up, and I had to stop for a minute to watch. Rabbi Steve Leder, author of *More Beautiful Than Before*, joined them, and he spoke of how important it is to find a silver lining in a hardship and how suffering transforms us. He said, "If you have to go through hell, don't come out of it empty handed." He recommended that we make note of the lessons we are learning and said it should be our mission to find the beauty in hardship and make something out of it. Tim McGraw was on the same show to discuss his new song release, "I Called Mama."

I googled Rabbi Leder and then saw that I missed the April 6th episode that he was on when he suggested that listeners stop for a minute and find a way to be productive for one hour rather than mentally catastrophizing the future in a panic. Exhale.

You were on my mind all day, Mom.

Love,

Wanting to Call Mama

Dear Roberta,

I woke up today to see the sun was shining through the living room windows. It's Sunday and I wanted to get the boys out, so we decided to take a wildlife refuge walk on the east end on Long Island, a suggestion from a friend. I don't remember the last time that we went to a public attraction like this without my having at least done a drive by to get my bearings first and try to anticipate any potential challenges and mitigate the unexpected. We didn't have the luxury of my taking a few hours to prepare first, so I thought it would be OK to wing it for once. After all, we are in a pandemic, and it should have been a "chill" day.

The plans were to stop at a local farmers market to see if they had cucumbers for Dimitri's garden and grab a hot dog or something light for lunch to hold us over until dinner at 5:30. We also had never been to the farmers market but, hey, it's just a farmers market, and I planned for a quick in and out.

The anxiety started building as soon as we left our driveway. SHIT. Why did I do this? The closer we got, the faster my heart was beating. What if? What if there was a long line that we couldn't manage? What if we had to turn around and go home, and there was a huge kerfuffle due to sudden plan changes? What if Maxx wouldn't get out of the van because it was a new place, so one of us had to manage the twins alone on a mile-long walk? Breathe.

We arrived at the farmers market, and it wasn't exactly what I had in mind. It was a few tents, mostly vendors selling items that wouldn't interest us like organic honey, vitamin supplements, or homemade pasta to cook at home. No cucumbers and certainly no hot dogs. However, there was a stand for one of our favorite bakeries that hires young adults with autism, so we grabbed several of their delicious brownies and then a loaf of bread from the Italian tent. I thought that might suffice for a snack until we got to dinner. No one liked the bread, but everyone had a brownie. SCORE! I started to feel slightly less anxious and actually empowered by taking everyone to a new place without planning. Step One accomplished.

Step two, the wildlife refuge walk. We pulled in, and it seemed as if there was a handicap space waiting just for us. We all got out of the van — SHIT! The damn ice cream truck. Mom, you know how much I loathe those trucks. Remember that summer when they were driving around our house over and over again like sharks because I couldn't get Michael to accept "No ice cream truck" without him tearing the house down? Those ice cream men loved us, but the feeling was not mutual. Sometimes we had to buy ice cream two times a day that year.

I told myself to breathe — it's OK, it's just the ice cream truck. Then . . . the unthinkable. Andrew said, "Damn it, we forgot to stop at the bank, and I don't have any cash." Oh man, everyone was out of the van and I knew this wasn't going to be pretty. I asked the driver if he only accepted cash, and he said, "Yes." Oh God. Michael was already starting to wind up and saying loudly, "It's bad news, it's bad news." I could see in Dimitri's eyes that he was also starting to wind up in response to Michael's tone.

Somehow, we got all three of the boys back in the van by telling them that there was an ATM two miles away. Dimitri corrected us that it was, in fact, 2.18 miles away. We assured them we would be back before 3:00 when he would be leaving. I begged the driver not to leave until we got back, and he agreed as long as it was no later than 3:15.

We got to the bank on Main Street, and we parked into what again seemed like our perfect handicap space. SHIT! It was right in front of a pizza place. Michael said, "Hey we forgot lunch. I want pizza." OMG. OK, I told myself to breathe again. I would just grab a few slices.

Andrew came out of the bank, and I told him that I needed twenty dollars to grab slices quickly. I waited in the short line that seemed like an eternity and she told me that they were only making entire pies and the wait would be twenty minutes. For the love of God! I begged her to please tell them to hurry, and she explained that she couldn't make a pizza cook faster. Like I didn't already know that. When I got ready to pay, she told me that they did not accept cash. Thank God that we have the close-by handicap space! I ran over, grabbed the credit card so as to not hold the line up, and finally paid. Out of the corner of my eye I saw two women my age sitting on Main Street drinking wine. I cursed them under my breath.

I returned to the van as if nothing was wrong at all, using my very calm voice that I have been coached to use at all times whether the sky seemed like it was falling or not. I saw Dimitri bouncing his leg and using his breathing exercises while looking at the time on his phone. I reassured him that it would be OK, that we were getting pizza for lunch and then ice cream for dessert and then going to the wildlife refuge. He kept saying repeatedly, "Sometimes things change, and that's OK." In my mind I was praying that Michael wouldn't snap because they were taking too long and cause a scene. He had been at his worst behavior right before quarantine, and there had been a few times when he had eloped from the house, and I was starting to have flashbacks. Maxx was spiraling into a giggling fit and Michael was yelling "Shut up, I'm hungry" at him.

Pizza was done, it was 2:55 and we were on our way back to the refuge. While Andrew drove, I passed back slices while praying that we wouldn't run into bad traffic on the 2.18-mile drive back. We arrived, the handicap parking place was still there along with the ice cream truck. The driver saw us so I knew that he was not going to leave. I still kept thinking about those two women drinking wine.

Ice cream was purchased, and we all got out of the van to what appeared to be a beautiful and serene attraction. There weren't a lot of people there, so it was easy to be socially distant. Dimitri and Michael walked ahead while Maxx was slightly reluctant as it was a new place, but he was smiling. Within five minutes, we were walking in the most tranquil, magical trail, and all five of us were enjoying every second. The more we walked, the better the experience. It was as if we were suddenly taken from a crowded, beyond bustling, over-the-top, hectic city to a serene country road. Dimitri was in heaven taking pictures for Instagram, and I even got a few pictures of us together.

It dawned on me that this was literally the first hour of time since the beginning of the quarantine in which we were enjoying ourselves as a family; we were all together, incredibly happy, and having fun. It's rare to find a place that all of us enjoy, given the combination of the three boys' unique challenges. This is definitely going to be at the top of our list of fun excursions, with a few small revisions planned for the commute.

It was a beautiful day Mom. I felt so grateful on the drive home.

Love,

Making Pandemic Memories

Dear Roberta,

This morning the quarantine truly brought us to our knees. We received a call at 5:00 a.m. with news that Andrew's father, Papou Bob, had passed away. Our hearts are broken. At the end of March he had fallen down a cement stairway and obtained spinal cord injuries. It seems so surreal that less than five months ago, he was dancing at Greek parties and embracing his fifteenth year as a volunteer on the Parish Council at our cherished church, The Greek Orthodox Cathedral of St. Paul. Ever since his retirement, he could be found there with a welcoming face, whether it was for weekly liturgies, christenings, weddings, or funerals. He never missed a Parish Council meeting and certainly wasn't shy in expressing his opinion on topics. My loving father-in-law, Papou Bob, is no longer with us. I still can't believe it. Andrew and I are in shock.

He somehow passed away in the middle of a pandemic without contracting the virus despite surgeries, hospitalization, and rehab during the quarantine. Andrew and I communicated with the surgeons and medical professionals on a daily, sometimes hourly basis. The emotional weight of the project of getting him the best rehab possible was so intense. It was our hope he could regain feeling in his paralyzed arms and breathe again after his injuries and post-accident tracheotomy. Being present as caregiver for both Papou and the boys was at the forefront of our days. We refused to believe that he wouldn't overcome; hundreds of people were praying for him, including priests around the country. While we got to see him on daily Zoom calls, it just wasn't the same as being there in person for him.

Our day was spent communicating the sad news with family and friends. There are no words.

Love,

*Hugging My Loved
Ones Closer*

Dear Roberta,

While our lives are certainly filled with surprises, planning a funeral in the middle of the pandemic certainly caught me off guard. Andrew and I have been communicating with the funeral directors and priests on the ever-changing guidelines for saying good-bye and burying a loved one during the pandemic. I always imagined a line of people coming down Long Beach Road to say good-bye at the funeral home and St. Paul's parish being left with standing room only for his funeral. I can't believe that we are sending him off with just a handful of people.

I am so panicked about childcare during the services. I need to have care for all three boys, in our tiny house, in the middle of the pandemic, for multiple hours at a time. Wow. Up until now, I have only allowed a few people inside of our home, and they are close assistants who we trust are following safety guidelines. Even so, they only come in and out to pick up or drop off one of the twins when taking them out in the community or to a state park for hiking or walking. I rarely leave Maxx with anyone for over three hours at a time, except with a very special loved one who cannot break quarantine due to underlying health conditions. I honestly started to consider having him sit in the van and watch movies and take walks in the funeral home neighborhood while Andrew and I take shifts during the wake and funeral. I called Keri, my coveted case manager within the autism moms community for help. I am so lucky to have her!

By early afternoon, Keri had screened potential matches, completed phone interviews, and recommended two people to support Maxx while Andrew and I coordinated arrangements for Papou's funeral services. It's Wednesday and the wake is on Friday night. Ugh. I still have to meet them in person. One of them lives near the funeral home, so I can't even believe that Andrew and I are going to interview him in the parking lot after we drop off Papou's suit. Pandemic at its finest.

Love,

Interviewing in
the Astoundingly
Nonoptimal Office

JUNE 19, 2020

Dear Roberta,

I remember Mother's Day when I wrote to you about how I was longing to be inside of St. Paul's. I never dreamt in a million years that the next time I entered the cathedral would be at Papou's funeral. Today, we walked inside for the first time post-quarantine, and Papou wasn't in his usual place to welcome parishioners. Yes, Anastasios from the Parish Council was there, but to me, the narthex was lonely and deserted. Papou wasn't there.

Other than at my wedding, I don't ever remember walking into church when he wasn't at the back of the church to greet us along with everyone else. He is known to everyone in the congregation for his "Welcome." As you know, church was incredibly important to him, and he took the position of welcoming everyone into our parish very seriously. Father Christopher talked beautifully about his need to connect people to each other based upon their individual backgrounds and of course his selfless dedication to the St. Paul community. As a member of the Parish Council, he was given a list of parishioners to call and check on during the quarantine. It appeared that he called everyone, literally hundreds of people, right before his accident. Everyone we spoke to and all of the social media posts had the same response: "I can't believe it! He just called me the other day, and we had a beautiful conversation." It was almost as if he received a subliminal message to connect with everyone he knew before his untimely passing.

Mom, I honestly felt like I was in another lifetime, and I was overwhelmed by emotions. I could feel your presence there too and knew that you were with me. Twenty-five people together with masks on at the front of our beautiful parish said their individual goodbyes to our beloved Dad, father-in-law, and Papou in the middle of the pandemic. I suddenly felt a river of sadness and exhaustion from the entire quarantine leading up to that moment just wash over me. Of course, the stress anticipating the week ahead was on my mind as well. I felt numb walking behind him as he exited St. Paul's for the last time.

We all headed to the cemetery. It was a gorgeous day outside, but the graveside service seemed so quick, isolated, and lonely. There were cemetery workers sitting in bulldozers waiting near us, literally watching for us to leave so that they could quickly close his grave. Still the sun was shining beautifully, and the sky was as clear and blue as his eyes.

On the way home, Andrew and I discussed how we planned to keep Papou's legacy alive, not only in St. Paul's, but in the Greek Orthodox community all over Long Island. It seemed surreal that we were sitting in the van together having a private conversation, something we rarely had time for pre-coronavirus, and yet we found ourselves alone, in the middle of a pandemic, in grief but in gratitude.

Love,

Learning From Papou

Dear Roberta,

It's official. The paperwork and approvals are complete. Admission day for Michael is on June 22nd. I just want to vomit every time that I think about it. I keep telling myself that I know it's the right decision for our entire family. Why does it have to be during a pandemic for Christ's sake? God grant me the serenity . . .

There is some improvement in the drop-off plan, to say the least. Michael and I are so beyond blessed in the process. Mom, I keep thinking back to the beginning of the quarantine when I told you that I knew I would be leaning on the autism agency throughout the pandemic and that they would again rise to the occasion of supporting our family during a crisis. They have, once again, brought me to my knees in gratitude.

Remember the original pick-up plan that I couldn't bear to think about? A group of support people from the school, mostly strangers, would arrive at our house one day, and I would have to explain to Michael that he was being transported to a new school where he would be living? The thought of that moment has been beyond heavy on my mind since I learned of the admission day process. For once, the coronavirus has played itself out in my favor.

Due to COVID-19 restrictions, staff from Michael's new school cannot enter our homes, and Michael cannot enter his residential house until he has been examined by their school nurse. That leaves the transportation piece back on our plate, which we know is impossible for safety reasons. Two of the senior behavior consultants who have worked with Michael for years, and might I add, whom he LOVES, will be driving him. Mom, when I heard this news I could not stop crying for hours, and I could hear you shouting, "Well Praise God!" The relief in my mind cannot be put into words.

Yes, there will still be a little dishonesty in the transportation plan, but safety is always the first and foremost concern. They have always coached me that if safety prevents me from carrying out a behavior plan, be safe first and then work on the plan and steps to avoid that situation in the future. It still breaks my heart into pieces that he thinks he is going on a field trip to Boston for being so successful in the Google classroom. He was, indeed, incredibly successful! He was a rockstar, Mom. He worked so hard in homeschool with his one-to-one behavior consultant teacher and didn't miss one single session. As a matter of fact, she even mentioned in our last meeting that she was challenged with coming up with enough work for him because he was zooming right through it all perfectly, without errors or difficult behavior. Bravo Michael!

I plan to drive to Boston separately, and when he arrives at the school, I will be there, along with kind, compassionate, and trained support and the senior behavior consultants that I have leaned on for years. It's not going to be easy by a long shot, but they have been our heroes during the pandemic for sure. Andrew and I decided to have large "Thank You for Being our Hero" signs designed and placed on the front of their property, a gesture that is not enough but that we hope begins to show them how much they mean to our family. You taught me how to say Thank You, two words that are powerful on their own and are even more transformational when paired with an act of gratitude.

Love,

Wishing I Could Say Thank You to Mom Again

Dear Roberta,

Tomorrow — Drop off day for Michael — Surprise — What if . . .? Ugh. These worries in my brain were so damn loud today that I wished for headphones. Mom, I wanted to turn it off, give everyone a happy day, get things done for tomorrow, go to bed. Today was Father's Day and the weather was gorgeous. While Andrew and I aren't in a celebratory mode, we went through the motions so that Dimitri and Michael aren't disappointed.

We headed to the beach with the boy's COMHAB workers and then went home for a BBQ, all while I discreetly finished the plan to move Michael to Boston tomorrow for his new residential placement. I need to have a secret bag packed so that I can quietly get up at 4:30 a.m. and exit the house quickly so that I don't wake anyone. The behavior consultants are all scheduled to arrive at 8:00 a.m. to surprise Michael with his "field trip" (aka safe drive) to Boston. I need to arrive at the school at least ninety minutes before them to sign papers and relax before he arrives to have "the conversation."

Mom, I haven't been able to pack one thing for him from home because he is home! Even on a day when things are "normal," if I move a pair of his shoes from one side of the room to another he notices and moves them back. In addition to the quarantined "secret packing project," remember we don't have access to any sites that have on-line ordering capabilities. I have literally been sitting in the backyard of our staff members Nick and Christian, using their laptop to order the items that Michael needs and having them shipped to the home of another staff member, Katie, who has been in charge of packing. Craziness as usual.

Before today, I haven't had one moment to actually see what Katie has done in the packing process. We just had minimal conversations that started and stopped at the drop of a hat about what I planned to send. She has the list of things that I need and has been communicating with me to find out if anything is missing. I headed over to her house alone before going to the beach to check on everything because Andrew will need to pick it all up later tonight after the twins are asleep. Mom, you should have seen the organization! I cried happy tears. I suddenly felt a mountain of stress melt off my shoulders. Everything was impeccable, packed in plastic crates, and perfectly labeled.

The beach trip was fabulous. Yep, the beautiful Atlantic Ocean was still there, and she looked gorgeous today! My thoughts frequently go back to our conversations about God's plan for me to marry someone who was from an area close to the coast 😊. How many times have I told you that I don't know how our family could function without the ocean? It is so calming, not just for the boys, but for all of us. All five! It's one of the very few places that we have where we all chill, relax, and almost always come home feeling rejuvenated. I am so thrilled that Michael will have access to the New England shores while attending his residential school.

I got super lucky today and finally connected by phone with my friend Barbara, who has three children with autism in separate residential schools on Long Island. We have been playing phone tag throughout quarantine because she is a nurse and I simply have not had a moment to speak on the phone. I knew exactly what I was going to hear — her own personal heartbreak as she and her husband have not had permission to spend time with their boys since day one of quarantine in March due to the lack of guidelines surrounding visitation with disabled loved ones in residential schools and group homes.

Despite the continuous social media activism and face to face protesting, the NY state government just hasn't responded. Even a precious video made by her son Anthony from his residential home, pleading with Governor Cuomo to let him and his brothers go home and swim in their pool received absolutely no response! We talked about her option to bring them home, but she and her husband are essential workers. There are no guidelines, so she and thousands of other parents and guardians like her don't know what to expect if they take their loved ones home. Will the agencies hold their placement? Will the students be able to return to their residential schools? Will the parents/guardians be able to care for their loved ones while holding down their jobs for a long period of time? What will the guidelines be, and when the hell are they going to suddenly appear? For Christ's sake, it's already three months into the quarantine, and we are already in Phase 2 of reopening. Barbara reminded me that the next protest at the state office is on Thursday, and I agreed to attend. My stomach is churning as I remember that I'm going to be in the same position as Barbara after tomorrow.

After we hung up, I realized that I had a long list of things to do before an early bedtime. I stayed super busy and said goodnight to the boys, knowing that the next time I will see Michael will be in Boston when I surprise him at his new school and tell him that this is where he is going to live for a while. I felt super motivated to just make it happen and move on to the next "whatever the new norm" is for our family. I have to leave at 5:00 a.m. hoping that no one will wake up. The behavior consultants are coming at 8:00 a.m. to pick Michael up.

As I lay my head down, thoughts of the May 27th Today Show episode with Rabbi Steve Leder, and his advice went through my mind again . . . "How I am Leaving the Pandemic." That day brought a surge of positive energy because the television background noise demanded that I stop everything to watch Rabbi Leder discuss how suffering can transform us. I thought of you and spent much-needed time praying. Praying for strength, resilience, and the will to press decline if Donna calls me tomorrow. She always seems to have a sixth sense about when I am the most vulnerable and decides that is the perfect moment to reach out with an enticing invitation.

I can only wonder what the pandemic may bring over the next few weeks, months, or even the next year for us. COVID-19, with its intimidating aura, continues to deliver surprises, bring a multitude of questions, very few answers, and a promise of unsteady moments. Your legacy of goodness, light, love and wisdom lives on while instilling the strength of a lion, courage to live one day a time, poise to walk gracefully (OK sometimes ☺), and last but not least, the burning desire to come out on top after a challenge.

Love,

Taking it one day at a time.

EPILOGUE

Dear Roberta:

I just got home from another Boston trip to see Michael. I am still only allowed to see him in a conference room for an hour, but yesterday we were also allowed to walk on the trail behind the school. Trips outside of his residence are not permitted yet, so as of now, the students are only allowed to go to the school building every other day. Mom, the school is just magical, and I am anxious for him to experience the program that Andrew and I saw at our pre-coronavirus visit. For now, I must trust that we made the right decision and respect the school's choice to err on the side of caution for the residential students. It's still heartbreaking to plan and participate in safe, socially distanced activities for his brothers here on our Long Island beach while knowing that he is still in quarantine and now in a different state. I visit him about every ten days, and yesterday, his treatment team brought up the idea of me visiting more often.

I usually make the trip to Boston alone as Andrew needs to stay at home to manage Dimitri and Maxx. The trips have given me the alone time that I have longed for since February, and Mom, it is just glorious! I have to admit that last night in the hotel, I was thinking about Donna a lot. I almost called her — no one would have known since I am in a different town where I don't know anyone.

Maxx's school decided to only provide a virtual summer program, and he does not fit the profile of a student that can learn in a virtual environment. Fortunately, he was approved to attend a specialized autism behavior clinic where he will receive one to one intense ABA therapy to treat and prevent further regression during the pandemic. After a lot of practice and positive reinforcement, he learned how to tolerate wearing a mask for an hour and was able to attend Papou's forty-day memorial service at St. Paul's church. There are no words to adequately express my gratitude to the people who made this all happen for him. He will also continue to have the village of support people in the afternoons and weekends, which means that we wear masks even within the walls of our own home. I continue to require consistent hand washing for anyone who enters our house, especially his treatment team members who stay for hours at a time. We are all on the honor program, and I trust that everyone will communicate if they don't feel well or were in contact with someone who has a confirmed case. I still worry a lot Mom.

The Suffolk JCC-Y stepped up to the plate yet again in the pandemic and delivered an exceptional five-week summer camp program for Dimitri. The smiles that I saw every day brought joy to my heart — finally he had a predictable day with structure again. It looks like he is headed back to school in the fall with a hybrid model of both in-person and virtual components. The high school program in our district provides an exceptional work-based learning environment for students like him who will not attend college. Historically, their day would include two to three hours of sampling various short-term jobs in the community. I wonder if this program will be included when he goes back in September. Oh, and the parents in my town were given an opportunity to vote on school bus transportation, and the majority opted out. This is going to be super interesting because the drop-off line at the high school usually stretches down the street on a non-pandemic day.

The twins turn eighteen in three weeks, and adult life is right around the corner for them. I need to start solidifying the housing and employment plans that I have for them. While the virus has plans on a soft pause for now, it's time to start moving forward. I don't want to jinx it yet, Mom, so I will tell you more when it looks like they are coming to fruition.

Through the whirlwind of non-stop days, I found time to work together with my manager and close friend, Elisa, to finalize another eBook in our job search series. We pivoted our book for females returning to the work force and wrote a book called *Landing an Internship Bootcamp*. In addition, I already started a new exciting project to help other recruiters and human resource professionals in their diverse and minority hiring process.

Mom, I decided to call a very coveted hair salon on Long Island to try being a redhead and was super lucky to get an appointment with the owner, Angela. Life is so funny sometimes with its twists and turns — I never put two and two together before that the name of the salon, "Hair Addict" references addiction in recovery. What an inspiring story Angela has with all of her personal and professional accomplishments during six years of sobriety. There are other hair stylists there, also in recovery, and I have made good friends with them as well. I have never had a sponsor or worked the steps from *The Big Book of Alcoholics Anonymous* and am planning to ask Angela to be my sponsor when I see her next week.

My thoughts these days seem to be consumed with fears of a possible second wave of the virus. I am so tired today, yet I still can't turn it off in my brain. Now I know what lockdown life for our challenged family looks like, and the thought of experiencing that again is terrifying. I don't know if I have the strength. Your presence has been one of the few, if not the only, things that got me through thus far. You coached me through achieving sobriety again and through a time of isolation, change, challenge, and motherhood that I never dreamt of. Even though you didn't experience a pandemic in your lifetime, you still knew how to guide me through. You taught me more in these past five months than I have learned in my entire life.

I have loved writing these impassioned and vulnerable letters to you. I hope there's not too much time before I write to you again.

Until the next time,

Leaning on Mom